GOD FOR NOTHING . . .

Richard MacKenna photograph by courtesy of The Guardian

GOD FOR NOTHING . . .

Is Religion Bad For You?

by

Richard MacKenna

CHURCHMAN PUBLISHING: Worthing 1986

GOD FOR NOTHING: Is Religion Bad For You?
by
Richard MacKenna
was first published in Hardback
by Souvenir Press Limited in 1984
First Paperback Edition
was first published in 1985 by
Churchman Publishing Limited
117 Broomfield Avenue
Worthing
West Sussex
BN14 7SF
Publisher: Peter Smith

Represented in Kingston, Ontario, Sydney and Wellington

Second Paperback Impression 1986
Third Paperback Impression 1987

ISBN 1 85093 019 8

Distributed to the book trade by:
Bailey Bros. & Swinfen Limited
Warner House
Folkestone
CT19 6PH

Made and printed in Great Britain by
Antony Rowe Limited, Chippenham

Contents

*For my mother, and in fondest memory of
Robert M. B. MacKenna, beloved physician*

Acknowledgements

Acknowledgement is gratefully made to publishers and individuals for permission to include extracts from the following copyrighted material:
The Royal Hunt of the Sun © Peter Shaffer Limited; *Amadeus* by Peter Shaffer, published by Andre Deutsch; *The Bell* by Iris Murdoch, published by Chatto and Windus; *Existentialism is Humanism* by Jean-Paul Sartre, published by Methuen, London; *We Are the Pharisees* by E.C. Hoskyns, published by SPCK; *Why I Am Not a Christian* by Bertrand Russell, published by George Allen and Unwin; *Autobiography* by Bertrand Russell, published by George Allen and Unwin; *The Art of Loving* by Erich Fromm, published by George Allen and Unwin; *The Farthest Shore* by Ursula le Guin, published by Victor Gollancz Ltd.; *The Velveteen Rabbit* by Margery Williams, reprinted by permission of William Heinemann Ltd; *Thus Spake Zarathustra*, Nietzsche, translated by Tille and M.M. Bozman, published by J.M. Dent and Sons Ltd.; *The Sign of Jonas* by Thomas Merton, published by Sheldon Press; *The Fire Next Time* by James Baldwin, published by Michael Joseph; *Markings* by Dag Hammarskjöld translated by W.H. Auden and Leif Sjoberg, reprinted by permission of Faber and Faber; extracts from 'The Love Song of J. Alfred Prufrock' and 'The Four Quartets' from *Collected Poems 1909-1962* by T.S. Eliot, published by Faber and Faber; extracts taken from *The Jerusalem Bible*, published and copyright 1966, 1967 and 1968 by Darton, Longman and Todd Limited and Doubleday and Co. Inc. and used by permission of the publishers; *The Voice of Experience* by R.D. Laing, published by Penguin Books Ltd., 1982; *A Portrait of the Artist as a Young Man* by James Joyce, published by Jonathan Cape Ltd., by kind permission of the

Executors of the James Joyce Estate; 'Death of a Salesman' from *Collected Plays* by Arthur Miller, published by Martin Secker and Warburg Ltd., © 1949 by Arthur Miller; *A View from a Broad* by Bette Midler, published by Sphere Books Ltd; extracts from the *New English Bible*, second edition © 1970 by permission of Oxford and Cambridge University Presses; *Man's Search for Meaning* by Viktor Frankl, reprinted by permission of Hodder and Stoughton Ltd; *The Sovereignty of Good* by Iris Murdoch, published by Routledge and Kegan Paul Plc; *Memories, Dreams, Reflections* by C.G. Jung, published by Pantheon Books; *The Development of Personality* and *Psychology and Religion* both by C.G. Jung, published by Routledge and Kegan Paul Plc; *Letters and Papers from Prison* and *Ethics*, both by Dietrich Bonhoeffer, published by SCM Press; *The Reality of God* by S.M. Ogden published by SCM Press; *Paths in Spirituality* by John Macquarrie published by SCM Press; 'Reflections on Gandhi' by George Orwell in *Collected Essays*, Vol IX published by Martin Secker and Warburg Ltd., © the estate of the late Sonia Brownell Orwell.

I am also most grateful to all those who have allowed me to mention their experiences. In order to avoid recognition of specific individuals, I have altered some of the details in certain cases.

Finally, heartfelt thanks to Sue, who typed, Robert, who read, and Tessa, who edited, without any of whom . . .

Prologue

Funeral visits are never easy at the best of times, but this one was a disaster. A distraught woman, with not the remotest interest in Christianity, confronted by a nervous curate with nothing helpful to say. Even then it might have been all right: at times like that he would try to help the mourner to express her grief – forget the Bible-thumping and be a catalyst to help the mourning process under way. Unfortunately a well-meaning friend of the widow was there too, obviously disconcerted at the lack of pious platitudes and lofty sentiments due from a cleric. As the widow's grief became more and more heart-rending and the curate's contribution seemed to extend only to holding her hand, the friend became restless, and tried to do the priest's job for him.

'Never mind, dear; after all, he's gone to a better place and it's selfish of you to cry. Just think of the love of God, and the Church.' Goaded by this well-meant irrelevancy and aware only of her desperate loss, the widow shouted at her friend, 'Fuck God and fuck the Church: they're good for nothing, I need John.' At least, she meant to say 'good for nothing', but under the pressure of the moment what she actually said was 'god for nothing'.

I've never forgotten that visit, partly because you don't forget sharing pain, but also because her words echoed beyond that particular situation. What is God good for, except to keep a few chinless clerics in employment? And sometimes when I get claustrophobia in church bookshops, surrounded by books with happy faces on the covers telling you how wonderful it all is, how God can make you clean, white and fragrant, and I look at the grey, frightened people in the shop and then at the real world rushing past outside, the little boy in me longs to cry out like the widow, 'F. . . God and F . . . the Church!', just to get some sort of human reaction, to

11

make people look up and *see*. Because God – the real God, not the God of pious bookshops – is too big, too dangerous, too disturbing to be fitted inside a dust-jacket at £3.50 a copy, or crammed into church between 10 and 11 on a Sunday morning. That is, if he's there at all. The widow cried out in anger and desolation, but was she crying out against someone – God – who had done something to her, or was she dismissing the whole thing as so much junk, irrelevant to her pain? *Are* God and the Church good for nothing?

If we took her at her word and decreed that all the churches and Christians should vanish overnight, what would happen? I have a secret fear that the only people to notice would be a few local conservation groups. Of course, advertisers would have to find some substitute for the joke parson to whom they resort so frequently, but would anyone else care? Certainly not the people who find Christians inward-looking, self-centred, parochial, smug; I don't just mean the ones who come along to barrack at midnight mass on Christmas Eve or who yell obscenities at me when I'm in my dog collar, but people like my agnostic or atheist friends who often seem to live more open, honest and loving lives than many Christians. As Bob Hope said, 'A zombie has no mind of his own and walks around without knowing where he's going or what he's doing . . . in Hollywood they call them "pedestrians".' In Britain we might call them 'The Church'.

And yet . . . and yet . . . for every ten clergymen sitting grinning vacuously over a cup of tea, there's probably at least one, unacclaimed, unrewarded, trying to bring life into deathly situations, working with the mad, the bad, the dying, the ill, the desperate, the afraid. And for every ten plaster-of-paris Christians, stiflingly proper and terrified to really *live* ('If Christians wish us to believe in their redeemer, why don't they look a little more redeemed?' asked Nietzsche), there must be at least one coping with doubt and uncertainty, trying to follow the desperately hard road of sacrificial love (that is, self-giving love, without demand or holding back). But which stands for truth?

One last image, that I hope you'll keep at the back of your mind throughout this book. If you imagine Brighton and Hove being built on the slopes of a volcano, you have a vague

idea of what the two Roman cities of Pompeii and Herculaneum must have been like, built on the slopes of Mount
Vesuvius. An estate agent's paradise – sun, sea air, lovely
views, ideal for a Roman retirement bungalow – except that
on 24 August AD 79 there was a vast explosion and the top of
Vesuvius was blown off. Pompeii was buried alive in lava and
many of its inhabitants choked to death by poisonous gases.
Herculaneum was buried in mud and lay undiscovered and
almost intact for about seventeen hundred years. I was being
shown round the excavated town by a distinguished historian
when he suddenly alarmed me by asking, 'Do you want to see
something very shocking?' C. of E. curates are a tough breed
nowadays, so after weighing the pros and cons of being
confronted by the phantom flasher of Napoli or getting my
hands on a lifetime's supply of feelthy postcards, I said yes.
Far from being shown the naughty murals of Pompeii – which
in their chauvinistic way the guides still won't let women see –
I was taken to an upstairs room and shown . . . a cross: quite
simply, carved on the wall of the room, a plain cross.

Now, sadly, a cross to a clergyman is about as shocking as
an invitation to a Mothers' Union coffee morning, and it took
some time for me to understand what the historian was getting
at, namely, the question of whether the cross was a Christian
symbol, or simply a decoration or something to do with the
structure of the room. If it *was* put there as a Christian
symbol, then it would have been something profoundly
shocking to the Roman eye: a symbol of a vicious and
degrading instrument of torture and death that was more an
embarrassment than a sign of victory to the early Church – it
was rather as if I were to put up a colourful poster of an
electric chair or gas chamber in my bedroom.

In fact it was the opponents of the early Church who were
probably the first to use the cross as a symbol – hence the
famous picture of the crucified man with the head of an ass.
The historian thought that the reality of the cross would be far
too shocking at that time for a Christian to carve it on his wall,
and that rather than being a symbol of Christ, it was more
likely a decoration of some sort. I sometimes wonder how the
many people who wear crosses as jewellery would feel if their
cross were replaced by a neat EPNS gallows. For them too,

the cross is a decoration, or at most a lucky charm. And for the Church?

And that is the image this book is trying to worry away at: is the cross a decoration or something more? Is God for nothing or everything? And you can't just nod vaguely and say, 'Oh yes, the cross is awfully important.' Like two silly girls I once heard at Speakers' Corner, heckling a man who was trying to talk to a small group about his real pain and doubt: 'Oh, but what about eternal life,' they kept chanting, as if they were talking about a clinic in the Midlands that they had read about that they hoped might patch him up. Because to be confronted by the cross, if we can stay with the image of Herculaneum, doesn't mean being shown something, like a tourist, and having it all explained to you in a guidebook so that you have it neatly filed away in your mind alongside the Sistine Chapel and a recipe for pasta. It means, initially, having to dig down through the centuries of accumulated mud and rubble, and then having to dig down through the years of accumulated apathy, laziness, defence mechanisms, habits, attitudes in oneself; and it can also mean perhaps, when the fragile surface of everyday living gives way, life precipitating one unwillingly down and down – and then to be confronted by what? A cross. But is the cross just a decoration, something carved on a wall, as relevant to real life as flock wallpaper? Or is it a signpost, something that points us to the deepest truth about the nature of reality, humanity – and God?

I'm not sure that I know the answer, and if I did I probably wouldn't feel the need to write this book. But then we shouldn't trust books that give easy answers; to find the truth for oneself is a very costly process, and no book can do the work for us. So if this book is more about questions than answers it's perhaps because of my feeling that it is in the very questioning that the meaning is to be found – 'You would not seek me, if you had not found me.' If a book can make one person feel the need to start on the long quest, then it has done its work. But if it stands there like an old nanny and says comfortingly, 'This is how it is', then although it may notch up record sales in religious bookshops throughout the length and breadth of the country, all it has really done is keep people

safely childish and sooths our age-old need for external
authority, for someone to tell us that thunderstorms are only
giants crashing tea-trays around in the clouds. Well, maybe
mustard-plasters and fairy stories can't help any more; maybe
we reach the stage of realising that not all the gurus or
sermons in the world can protect us in the end from our own
pain and loneliness, from the need to take responsibility for
our own lives, to start that slow and painful process of digging
down into ourselves, like the explorers of Herculaneum, and
finally facing what confronts us at the bottom – the cross of
meaning or meaninglessness. And it is a journey that we must
make alone: alone before God – or nothing.

One last word of warning: 'Would any of you think of
building a tower without first sitting down and calculating the
cost, to see whether he could afford to finish it? . . . Or what
king will march to battle against another king, without first
sitting down to consider whether with ten thousand men he
can face an enemy coming to meet him with twenty
thousand?' (Luke 14: 28ff.). Truth *is* costly but, as Montaigne
said, we are born to inquire after truth, even though 'it
belongs to a greater Power to possess it'. In other words,
maybe we are born to seek for what we can never find, and
yet, as G.E. Lessing said, 'it is not through the possession of
truth, but through the search for truth', that the worth of a
man lies; not in what he knows, but in the efforts he has made
to know it; 'If God were to hold out enclosed in His right hand
all truth, and in His left hand the everlasting active desire for
truth, although with the condition that I should remain in
error for ever, and if He said to me: "Choose!" I should
humbly take His left hand and say, "Father, give! The
absolute truth is for you alone".'

1. Life is a four-letter word

But where to start the search? In the past, perhaps, we could
have begun by drawing a map of heaven and a portrait of
God, and gone on from there. But since we don't even know
if they are there in the first place, it would surely be
dangerous to begin a journey by building castles in the air;
and confronted by the great theological structures of the
past, perhaps many of us feel, with Prospero, that:

> These our actors
> As I foretold you, were all spirits and
> Are melted into air, into thin air:
> And like the baseless fabric of this vision,
> The cloud-capp'd towers, the gorgeous palaces,
> The solemn temples, the great globe itself,
> Yea, all which it inherit, shall dissolve
> And, like this insubstantial pageant faded,
> Leave not a rack behind. We are such stuff
> As dreams are made on, and our little life
> Is rounded with a sleep.

As Prospero found, after the visions are faded and Ariel,
Caliban and the spirits have all left the stage, you are left
with, quite simply, man. And it is with man that the search
must begin, because 'man', to be human, is all that we really
know, the only fact that we really have to work on; man, the
'stuff as dreams are made on' – visionary, but also dreamer,
and whose life is 'rounded with a sleep' – in other words,
man who can be certain of only one fact in his life: that he
will die.

So I would like to start the search in Covent Garden, not to
sing a rousing selection from *My Fair Lady*, but because
that's where my office was when I worked on the problem

page of Britain's second-largest women's magazine. Now
women's magazines may seem sad creatures when encountered dog-eared and two years out-of-date in the dentist's
waiting room, but in many ways they are a helpful mirror of
modern life. To begin with, there is the striking cover,
usually with a picture of a well known personality. 'Paul
Newman,' the headline screams, 'How He Keeps Those
Good Looks. You Thought They Were Natural?' And the
Royal Family are great favourites for hot-selling magazine
covers. But whoever the personality on the cover, the idea
seems to be that our own lives are somehow dull and
uninteresting – that we need to live vicariously through
someone larger than life – more attractive, richer, more
intelligent.

I meet the same attitude when people discover I was once
an actor – 'Oh, have you met X or Y? What's he/she *really*
like? What was he/she wearing? What did you talk about?'
and so on. These token people become invested with almost
magical properties. Perhaps most hideous of all are the
braying parasites you find littering the gossip columns and
society pages, but *someone* must be interested in them, feel
excited at the thought of them – want to be like them.
Perhaps this is the heart of the matter: that we feel so
inadequate in ourselves, so unlovely, so unlovable, that we
want to be these other shinier people, even though we
probably know that in reality they are no different from us,
and that when Vivien Leigh was finally kissed by America's
sweetheart, Clark Gable, all she could think about was the
taste of his false teeth. Or is the truth even darker, that by
living through others we avoid having to face ourselves and
the problem of our existence?

So much for the cover and the beautiful people. Inside the
magazine you are probably struck first by the glossy and
inviting advertisements. Inviting they may be, but in their
subtle way they too tell us that something is rotten in our
own particular state of Denmark. Unlike the cover, they
promise the possibility of change. After all, no one can
suddenly develop eyes as blue as Paul Newman's, but by
changing your brand of vodka you may make your guests
respect you more, or by changing your brand of scent you

may make yourself more seductively beautiful, or if you feel
you're an inadequate mother perhaps you can prove you
really love your family by washing their whites whiter –
without having to boil-wash, of course. Whatever they're
about, the advertisements promise the chance of bettering
oneself and one's life through grabbing on to externals – the
accessories that surround us and by which we define
ourselves in competition with our neighbours, or simply
because that's the only way we can value ourselves. What
sort of statement about her life was the American woman
making, who asked to be buried sitting in her sports car? But
the ads keep niggling at us, suggesting that there is a better
way, that if we only get this for our very own, then we will be
happy at last. The more you have, the safer you will be.

After the advertisements, the fashion and beauty tips, and
helpful articles about the home (fifty ways to stay out of the
kitchen this Christmas), you come to the short stories and
serials, a seductive world that seems to obey very different
laws from our own, a world where you can be absolutely
certain that no matter how ghastly the ordeal the hero and
heroine have to undergo, Love Will Find A Way. It's a very
warm and comforting environment to wander through but,
quite apart from the rose-coloured glasses, it can create
major problems if taken seriously.

Like any system that sees life in terms of big, undefined
concepts like Love, Duty, Passion and Destiny, and where
our motives and character are sharply delineated in black
and white, it is a hopeless schooling for reality. Very often
the victims whose sad letters would arrive for the problem
page were people who had learned to see life in romantic-
fiction terms and had then been overwhelmed by the sheer
grind of reality and the ambiguity of their own emotions,
which simply wouldn't fit neatly into little boxes labelled
'Love' or 'Eternal Unity'. But the vast sales of identikit
romantic novels show that there is a huge demand for the
reassuring vision of a world where things turn out all right in
the end. The hero's feet never smell, and if he snores he
does it endearingly. The heroines never get dandruff and
seem blithely immune to the 'times of the month'. Babies
are always beautiful, and Love, when finally triumphant, is a

glorious destiny that will put hero and heroine into a sort of joyful suspended animation until death (which of course, is never mentioned) when, presumably, they both cease together on the midnight with no pain.

It may seem cruel to knock these innocent escapist fantasies, but like the obsession with beautiful people and the advertisements, they seem to point away from the basic problem of coming to terms with reality and with oneself. You can live vicariously through others, you can try to change the externals of your life by building ever bigger and better cocoons, you can find a respite from the footslogging of life by becoming a beautiful Regency orphan girl (or James Bond or Superman), but sooner or later these escape routes become as flimsy as the magazine they are printed in, and then you end up at the back on the problem page. You'll notice that I haven't mentioned the religious chat, usually tucked away on a quiet page if it's there at all, and manned by photogenic or fatherly figures, nor the few lines of Uplifting Verse about how it helps if you believe; but somehow they seem as relevant or helpful as an article written in Esperanto. They can't stop the inexorable drift back to the problem page.

Now, problem pages or agony columns are always good for a cheap laugh at parties, but they fulfil a very important service. Every week hundreds of letters arrive, not for publication, and a small team of dedicated people write personal replies in the name of whoever heads the column in the magazine or newspaper. These letters run the gamut from teenage sleepless nights over Barry Manilow to desperate problems of death, madness, alcoholism, child-battering – you name it. But what makes people write to a total stranger, rather than seek help nearer at hand? Partly, perhaps, it is because for regular readers the face at the top of the page and the printed replies become like a familiar friend who can be trusted. But also, perhaps, because of the deep sense of isolation in which many people suffer. I say *in* which they suffer because as well as suffering from isolation, many people, even in large family or friendship groups, find that, when confronted by a major problem, they are suddenly alone and have to reconsider relationships they had previously taken for granted. In the light of the cancer in my womb, I begin to see the husband I have lived with for twenty years as a stranger; my marriage is empty, my wife and sons bore me, but could I really trust good old Jack, or anyone else for that matter, with such emptiness? And so people turn to a stranger in a letter, where there can be no embarrassing conflict between the real self and the projected image.

Perhaps isolation itself, that crippling sense of being alone, is the main culprit. We are surrounded by people almost all the time, and yet we feel alone. And then when we are alone, we feel the need for people to fill the gap – the gap we know from experience they can't fill. And so we slog on with our lives of quiet desperation, although our defences against reality are so strong that it often takes a problem to make us realise how desperate we are. And so the letters come flooding in, thousands of them every year, from men and women of every race, religion and background. Ordinary people, not freaks, burdened with troubles that make nonsense of the bright world of the cover, or the short story or the advertisements. And often there is little that can be said in reply, except possibly to put the person in touch with a local helping agency.

But who could help the woman who had just been told by her doctor that she'd got three months left to live? Or the woman caught in the living death of a marriage where the only time she saw her husband was at midnight when he'd fall into bed dead drunk. The reason she wrote initially was to ask for advice about clearing the bedroom of the terrible smell of urine – the husband was so drunk every night that he would wet the bed in his sleep. But in the course of the letter the whole horrible story came out: the penal servitude of a marriage spent cleaning up the morning after, washing, cooking, trying to protect the kids, enduring sex on demand or getting a fist in the face; no love, no support, no friendship – a beast of burden, good for cooking, cleaning and opening her legs; but not complaining, because she had lost all sense of her own worth. She just endured, without hope or chance of escape.

When I started work in the personal correspondence

section of the problem page, my wise and compassionate boss said that, if our replies did nothing else, they should make the person who received them feel that they mattered – that they were important. This may not sound very much, but it points to one of the great problems of modern man: not only does he feel isolated and lonely, but he lacks any sense of self-value. Hence, perhaps, the great emphasis we put on success and achievement. We value ourselves in terms of what we can do or what we can buy. The people who queue up to make it into the *Guinness Book of Records* are only a grotesque extension of this – 'I may not be valuable or important in myself, but at least I'm the only person in the world who can eat two million frogs' legs in an hour.' But the astonishing thing about the really successful people I've met is that they all confess to a fear of being found out. No matter how successful they are or how solidly that success is rooted in genuine achievement, they have a fear of being seen through, as if what they had done was somehow not enough, that somewhere there was an un-healed little child looking through those famous eyes. And the West's great problem of unemployment is increased by our sense that self-worth is given by what we 'do' – no job, no worth. But with or without jobs there's a feeling that we have to cover up, to hide or disguise large parts of our personalities – the very word person comes from the Latin for an actor's mask – and the more entrenched we become behind our mask, the lonelier we feel and the more worth-less, because only *we* know the truth of the face behind the mask.

All this is bound up with the third problem that came up time and time again in the letters. Like the feelings of isolation and lack of self-value, it seemed to underlie so much of what one sees when working in mental hospitals, researching for advertising, counselling, or working in parishes. It's the fact that people find it very difficult to love – *really* love – or be loved. We try, God knows we try, in fact many of us spend our lives in pursuit of love – or rather, of the experience of being loved. Because here again it comes back to that need to feel a sense of value, and by feeling that we are loved we try to make up for that lack of love we feel for ourselves. But the sort of love we often give or receive is more like a bargain than a gift: two masks look at each other and reckon up what they need – there are strings attached, of course, because only a fool gives something for nothing, even in love.

But this is still only scratching at the surface, dealing with symptoms of a greater disease. As the rather cynical Doctor Harley, we'll call him, of the medical advice page, once remarked to me as I complained about the unfairness of some terminal illness,'Ah, but you've got to remember that life itself is a fatal disease that no one recovers from.' Indeed, although we scramble desperately to forget it. Once in New York I got all dressed up, borrowed some money and went to sample the Oak Room at the Plaza Hotel, a sort of posh version of our Savoy Grill Room in London. At the bar I got talking to a New Yorker who was a typical product of the American dream. From a poor family, he'd worked his way to the top and now controlled a large magazine syndicate. Beautiful wife, beautiful house on Long Island, beautiful cars, beautiful children – he had it all. Except that he was sitting in the Oak Bar getting plastered because something had happened to make him question all he stood for. A few days previously, a young man driving a sports car had cornered too sharply on the road by his house, and the car had smashed through the fence and rammed into a tree. My friend had never seen a dead body before, let alone a mutilated youthful one, and for the first time in his life he was suddenly confronted with the fact of death, with the fact that, one day, he would be carted off to the mortuary too. And in the light of the young man's smashed-in face, all his beautiful belongings – wife, children, house, cars and so on – had turned to dust.

We all suffer from this fatal disease of life, and yet society does everything in its power to make us forget that sooner or later we come to the end.

We're none of us ready for death, we thrust it out of our consciousness; one of the most tragic things about so many funerals is not just the sense of shock at the terrible intruder, reminding everyone of their own mortality, but also the sense of lost time, of missed opportunities. We live as if we were immortal, but time is not on our side; by the time the funeral comes, it's too late to say, 'If only . . .' But the real problem of death concerns not sadness or a sense of loss, not even our own mortality: it is to do with the question that mortality asks us – what, after all, is this whole rigmarole about? Are we born just to die, and does that inevitable death make all our achievements, our dreams, hopes, loves and longings of as much worth as an empty cigarette packet? At the end of the game, says the Spanish proverb, king and pawn go back into the same box. The last words of Brian Piccolo, the American professional footballer, as he died of cancer were, 'Can you believe it, Joy? Can you believe this shit?'

The French, as always, have a word for it: the absurd. The absurdity of man with his immortal longings, his need for permanence and purpose and his aspiration toward love, in this impenetrable, purposeless universe. By some freak of nature an ape learned to walk upright, to talk, to think, to dream, to create – and to be aware of the fact that it must die. And in the light of death, all our hopes and dreams and longings become absurd, a tragicomedy with a very bitter taste. 'When we are born,' wrote Shakespeare, 'we cry that we are come to this great stage of fools' (*King Lear*). Man postures in an empty theatre, trying to follow a script he can only guess at, knowing that sooner or later the curtain must fall.

This lack of meaning, that seems to make all our lives signify nothing, was explored by Albert Camus, the French writer who called the human condition 'absurd'. And like Shakespeare he used a theatrical image to describe our existence. Normally we are unaware of the absurd nature of our situation because we are shackled to our superficial lives by 'la chaîne des gestes quotidiens', the chain of our everyday life in all its details, but there are moments when 'les décors s'écroulent' – a terrifying image – when the scenery of our little play suddenly crashes to the ground and we are left alone on stage, overwhelmed by the senselessness of our daily routine, our existence. 'The bright day is done, and we are for the dark.'

Just as with the explorers at Herculaneum, this is the cross that faces us at the end of all our excavations – meaning or meaninglessness; 'life is a useless passion,' said Sartre, or is it? By starting with the problem page and then talking of funerals, I've rather assumed that we normally reach the cross more or less by accident, like Alice falling down the rabbit hole. But if we are not propelled down the hole by force of circumstance, then we can find a multitude of ways to board over the cracks; we will gladly let ourselves be enslaved 'the chain of our everyday habits', to keep us from the vertiginous free-fall. If we ever stopped to think for long enough, then we would become aware of our 'infinite longing, and the pain of finite hearts that yearn', and this would lead to deep anxiety. So what do we do instead? I've often been intrigued by mankind's long-standing need to carve initials on buildings and monuments; I think it's in Pompeii that some ancient Roman scrawled a poem which goes something like, 'I wonder, o wall, that your stones do not fall, so scribbled upon by the nonsense of all.' But has the 'nonsense' actually got something to do with our need for permanence, our sense of time passing and our desire to leave something of ourselves behind? The same sometimes applies when people have children. And this struggle for survival takes many forms.

I've called them 'boarding over the cracks', exercises in preventing anxiety, but they are also products of man's desire for unity with something other/greater than himself, and if the two ideas seem contradictory or not quite connected, that's because the view you take depends on the balance of meaning versus meaninglessness in your particular equation; they may give us a clue to the meaning of existence, or they may simply confront us with its lack of meaning – its absurdity.

Materialism we have already considered when looking at the ads in the magazine, but it's perhaps worth emphasising (again) what a pervasive creed this is in Western society, how happiness becomes equated with 'having' and taking things for one's very own. Of course man needs to 'have' a certain number of things, a certain standard of living, before he can start to realise his potential, but the other side of the coin is the danger that he will only understand his potential in terms of how much he can 'have'. Surrounded as we are by belongings, it is as if we cease to 'have' them, and they start to 'have' us; they become all-important to us, we define ourselves in terms of them, and in the end they swallow us up (just as we have swallowed up so much in our frantic desire for more). The effect of this is to alienate us from our fellow man because he is a potential rival, and from the world itself because we no longer see ourselves as part of it or respect its rights in itself (and our role as stewards of those rights); instead we see the world as an 'it', a thing, an object to gratify our desires.

Finally we are alienated from our very selves because we have surrendered our freedom of being to a compulsion: we cannot respect anything or anybody in their own right – they have to belong to us. Witness the frightening parties one sometimes blunders into, where the conversation revolves entirely around possessions – the new Rover, new video machine, new house, new wife (better window-dressing than the last model), new holiday – new everything except renewal of ourselves. No change, growth, hope, love. At the risk of sounding like a romantic novelist, I would like you to take all these unexamined terms on trust for the moment: can we simply say that on the side of meaninglessness one can see how materialism can rob man of any meaning except as a potentially dangerous junk-shop, like the white hunter who has to kill an animal and mount it on his wall before he can appreciate it, but on the side of meaning, our very aversion to this suggests we may feel that man has some other destiny.

Besides the romantic stories in the magazines, there's another sort of love story which is a particular twentieth century speciality – narcissism. 'You're a narcissist,' said the Monty Python character coming upon his colleague gazing rapturously into a mirror. 'No I'm not,' came the angry reply, 'a narcissist is someone who has a foolish infatuation with himself, but this is the real thing.' And for many of us today, Me, I, Self, Myself Personally, *is* the only real thing, the sole criterion by which we apprehend the world and consider its contents, and phrases like 'because I felt like it' or 'because I want to' fill the air.

Now narcissism is as common in the religious life as elsewhere, as we struggle to perfect ourselves; and just as in the gym you find the body-builders gazing earnestly at themselves in the mirror, straining to develop perfect 'glutes' or 'pecs' or 'bis', so the religious scene is littered with people who are in danger of replacing God with self-culture, anxiously watching themselves for signs of growth and grace. And so we shop around for a better church, better denomination, better religion, or even anxiously seek out religious books that will give us all the answers in exchange for the purchase price. Perhaps this is what Robert Merton, the great contemplative writer, meant when he said, 'I have renounced spirituality to find God.' Narcissism doesn't recognise any stronger commitment than one's duty to oneself, and so love for God or life or other people is only viable so long as it is seen to be paying dividends. And when I get bored with God, my marriage, my mistress, my obeying the law, my pregnancy, my anything, then I dump them because 'I'm not getting anything out of it/him/her/them'.

One of the signs of the immature personality is the inability to defer gratification – 'I want it, and I want it *now*.' If one is indulging in narcissism, then the present moment becomes all-important, and one's own wishes are always the prime consideration. The most real thing in the world is *me*, and what is outside me is only real in so far as I want it or need it. In fact this state is very similar to that of the baby, its reality revolving around warmth and the breast; and so for us the world itself becomes a big breast which we demand must suckle and pleasure us with people, cigarettes, drink, sex, religion. But if you meet people who are so completely turned in on themselves, or if you follow the road of self far enough, there is always a bleak sense of dissatisfaction and also a feeling of loss – as if you have lost something of what it is to be human. In the end, you find yourself alone in a desert of your own making. Rather like Las Vegas – a garish pleasure-dome stranded in the desert, full of isolated people desperately pulling the handles of the one-arm bandits in the hope that life will pay out. Some people go mad when they win the jackpot. Others wear gloves to stop their fingers bleeding from constantly feeding the machines from their baskets full of nickels. Which is more a desert – the place or the people?

There is another escape from anxiety that moves in the opposite direction from self. We can shed our fears and anxiety about our personal existence by surrendering our being to the group. This must appeal to something deep-rooted in our heredity – man hunting in packs and staying in the tribal group to protect himself from the night and the tiger. Writers who have tried to analyse the fascist regimes of Germany, Italy and Spain, put down their popular appeal to a deep longing for security. Even when it becomes like a gaol, people may prefer the sense of order, direction and security that the state can give, to the freedom that causes fear and anxiety. Paul Tillich saw the rise of German fascism as a surrender to authority: 'A freedom that leads to fear and anxiety has lost its value; better authority with security than freedom with fear!' And Herbert Matthews wrote about Italian and Spanish fascism: 'Fascism was like a jail where the individual had a certain amount of security, shelter and daily food.'

One doesn't have to look far to see the similarities with today's totalitarian regimes. I remember queueing to see Lenin's tomb in Moscow. As a tourist you can jump most of the mile-long queue of people visiting the shrine, but you cannot miss the atmosphere of devotion as they prepare to enter the still centre around which their universe revolves. While I was inside the tomb, down the long flights of steps in the refrigerated presence of the mummified idol, a Russian woman started to shout something. The reaction amongst her fellow Russians was electric – rage, panic, fear – as if someone had said the roof was falling in. But the guards are well schooled for this sort of eventuality and, neatly reversing his rifle to butt uppermost, one of them clipped her under the jaw and knocked her unconscious. Her body was removed, and with a deep feeling of relief the ceremonial file-past resumed. Devotion to a political cause or system helps us find a purpose amidst the confusion and emptiness.

And what was the man saying about his life, who wanted his ashes scattered at the goal-mouth of his football team? 'People love slavery and authority,' wrote Nicholas Berdyaev; 'the mass of mankind has no love of freedom, and is afraid of it.' In my parish (and in post-imperial Iran) you find young Iranian girls eager to adopt the traditional headscarf: to us, the symbol of an outdated and feudal concept of woman, to them the symbol of a clearly defined and limited

role with a minimum of freedom and a maximum of directedness. And, tragically, some of the battered wives who used to
write to me were more frightened of unguided freedom away
from home than of their life of broken arms and ribs and the
rape of themselves, and sometimes their children, by their
brutalised husbands. Better the devil you know. . .

Package tours, rugger clubs, trade unions, church congregations, men's clubs, women's clubs, political parties, the
forces, the old-school tie, all give us a meaning and help us to
define ourselves in a way that risks being little different from
Neanderthal man huddled round the fire in the cave with his
tribe, frightened of the dark outside. The risk of the group is
that man sacrifices his unique personality, but there is an
equivalent risk to the group or community if man pursues
individuality without any guide or reference point beyond his
own need or desire for individual fulfilment. Risking a crude
generalisation, you might say that the two sides can be seen in
America and Russia. In a totalitarian regime the individual is
seen as dangerous, and group values are paramount; the
search for individual truth leads to labour camps and psychiatric wards. In America, on the other hand, social analysts are
beginning to worry about the effects of the explosion in the
Sixties and Seventies of the cult of self-fulfilment, self-
actualisation, self-expression, call it what you will. New York
police say that increasing numbers of drivers simply ignore
red lights, halt signs and so on – a symptom of the way in
which people cease to feel any sort of obligation to the group:
their own wishes are paramount.

The conflict here is between the fact that man the individual
exists in a community, is a social animal with obligations to
others, and yet that the community, the system, can take on a
life of its own and in its own interests (power, survival)
oppress the very human values that it was created to protect.
Revolutionaries may not care to remember that it was the
murdered Spartacist leader Rosa Luxemburg who attacked
Lenin and the Bolsheviks for their suppression of independ-
ence:

Freedom for the supporters of the government only, for
members of one party only – no matter how big its

membership may be – is no freedom at all. Freedom is always for the man who thinks differently. This contention does not spring from a fanatical love of abstract justice, but from the fact that everything which is enlightening, healthy and purifying in political freedom derives from its independent character, and from the fact that freedom loses all its virtues when it becomes a privilege.

But worship of the self can also take on a life of its own and suppress human values. An Englishman on holiday in California was walking along the beach dressed in blazer and grey flannel trousers. He was astonished to be greeted with hostility and cat-calls: 'Hey man, you belong like in the zoo, man – you're in prison, man, we're all free and mellow and laid back.' The Englishman replied that he felt that he was really the freest person there, because he was dressed as he liked to be and unconcerned about what effect he might have, whereas the people who took such exception to him were unable to cope with his individuality and were actually asking him to adopt the same uniform attitudes and appearance as themselves, before they could accept him. Their very obsession with individuality had become a uniformity. The individual who is solely concerned for himself is a dangerous creature because he acknowledges no obligations to his fellow creatures, and yet it is in answering such duties, in recognising and tending the needs of others, that man seems to achieve his unique individuality and freedom: freedom from the dominance of self, freedom to be open to others.

And where does this tension between individual and community fit into the equation of meaning or meaninglessness? On the side of meaninglessness, we see how man can slip into being less than fully human, either by surrendering his individuality and anxiety about personal existence to the group or by pursuing the vision of self at the expense of others. But on the side of meaning, we need to be able to stand back and assess both the group and the individual against different, admittedly vaguer, concepts, such as freedom and duty. Man is more important than the group; there are values more important than Me, and my very obsession with My Freedom can make me less than free.

One last very primitive way in which we paper over the cracks. The anthropologist might call them orgiastic states; in London or New York they are called sex'n'drugs 'n'rock 'n'roll. Easy to look down our well-bred noses, but apart from the obvious turn-on of pleasure, surely these rites show a desperate craving for unity with something more than oneself. Caught up in the moment of orgasm or the high or the blast of the music, the terrible sense of separateness and aloneness disappears, we are taken out of ourselves, at one with something greater. How else to explain people like my friend who, despite catching endless social diseases, returns night after night to one of the raunchier West End clubs? Or the girl who, despite knowing all the dangers, found her life revolving more and more around the needle and the vein? Or the kids at the heavy metal concert I went to, shaking their heads and bodies in a frenzy as the grotesquely over-amplified music battered their ear-drums and their senses, at the risk of their hearing? (It took me two days to lose the partial deafness and ringing in the ears caused by the music.) If you feel superior to all this, have you never known the pleasant feeling when drinking, as the alcohol starts to take over your system, leaving you feeling somehow freer and lighter? There's not that much difference.

All these reactions to anxiety, these exercises in escapism, move in one of two directions. Either they distance us from accepting responsibility for ourselves, by involving the group, materialism and so on, or they take the form of looking for something more in life, like pleasure or personal growth. In all these forms of escape that we have looked at, there has been movement, even if it's only backwards to the comfort of the womb. I said at the start of the chapter that being human is all we know, but this movement suggests 'being human' is not a static concept but a dynamic one, with the possibility of change and growth or the counter-possibility of falling away and diminution. So the tension of meaning versus absurdity, positivity versus negativity, is there even in the routes we follow to escape from that tension. But if we try to be honest with ourselves and to confront the problems of existence head-on, the picture is still very ambiguous.

Classical myths are full of images of the hero having to

travel between two opposing points, each of which is equally deadly – the man-defeating rocks through which Jason had to pass, or Scylla and Charybdis, the monster and the whirlpool between which Odysseus had to find his way home. And in our search for what it means to be human, we too have to find our way between the contradictions that make up our lives. 'What a piece of work is a man!' said Hamlet, 'How noble in reason! how infinite in faculty! in form, in moving, how express and admirable! in action how like an angel! in apprehension how like a god! the beauty of the world! the paragon of animals! And yet, to me, what is this quintessence of dust?' The author of the second creation story in Genesis saw the same duality: 'The Lord God formed man of dust from the ground, and breathed into his nostrils the breath of life; and man became a living being.' Man comes into being through separating himself from the world of things; he is no longer just a part of nature, and no longer totally subject to nature's laws. Other creatures adapt themselves to their environment – man adapts his environment to himself. In a sense, man transcends nature; he is not simply what he is, plain old Joe Bloggs, but he is also possibility, all that he may be or become.

We have seen how difficult it is to say what being 'human' means because, far from being ready-made, it is incomplete, yet to be attained. A cat is a cat, but *we* are offered a myriad different possibilities of being and acting, and we have to find the right path or risk falling away from all that we might be. My grandmother could have been another boring/bored gentlewoman, but in the teeth of family and social opposition she fought to become one of the first women doctors. The son of a minor public family in Florence fought against family snobbery to join the 'working classes' and become Michelangelo, sculptor. His four massive sketches for *The Slaves*, now in the Florence Accademia, are unfinished, and the impresssion they give is of raw, vibrant life struggling to emerge from the dead stone, massive bodies trying to heave themselves out of the marble – man and spirit in revolt against matter. Michelangelo called them 'pure exhalations of life emerging from the destruction of the matter'. In the same spirit, Sartre talks of man sculpting his life: 'To begin with he

is nothing. He will not be anything until later, and then he will
be what he makes of himself . . . Man is nothing else but that
which he makes himself.' From the dust, from the dead
marble, emerges a being.

But man is not completely free. The slaves struggle to
emerge from the stone, but it still retains them. Man, with
the breath of life in him, has freed himself of many of
nature's laws, but he is still determined by them. We do not
ask to be born; we do not ask to die. And there is a
givenness about our situation that we can never completely
overcome. I may want to be another Michelangelo but I
have neither the talent nor the genius. I may be an Afghan
tribesman with a dream of freedom, but I choke to death in
Russian chemical rain. Perhaps like Troilus I may want to
show the height and depth of my love and find that 'this is
the monstruosity in love, lady – that the will is infinite and
the execution confined: that the desire is boundless and the
act a slave to limit'. Or perhaps, like Troilus, I may find that
the one on whom my life is fixed is nothing but a whore. So
we stand confronted with all the possibilities of our existence
and yet limited by all the 'givens' in our situation – family,
race, society, intelligence, our place in history, our well
established patterns of behaviour, the irrational in us – all
the many hidden motives and pressures of the subconscious
that make it almost impossible for any act to be simple: 'for I
do not do the good I want, but the evil I do not want is what
I do' (St Paul to the Romans).

But supposing that, despite the pressure of the past and
the given, I am prepared to stand in the tension that exists
between the openness of the future and the closedness of the
past (not one iota of which I can change) and face the
challenge of finding myself, what then? Panic, basically. 'To
be free,' said Sartre, 'is to be condemned to be free.' And we
have come back full circle to all the escape routes we use to
evade anxiety – but this time, the anxiety of freedom.
Because if I am free, I am free to make mistakes, to make
the wrong decisions and choices. Like Portia's suitors forced
to choose between the three caskets, once you've made your
choice you cannot go back; the other two caskets, and
whatever they might have contained, are closed to you for

ever. Where would I be now, what would my life be like, if I had stayed on the problem page and never become a priest? Michelangelo called his sculptures 'life emerging from the destruction of the matter', and destruction is the dark and frightening side of creativity. If I accept my freedom then that will involve destroying old patterns in myself and progressively letting go of all that I have clung to from my childhood: something in the past must be allowed to die, so that something may be born in the present.

In the same way, as we move through the various cycles of life – childhood, adolescence, early adulthood and so on until the final preparation for death – we need to accomplish the tasks set us by each cycle, otherwise they will return to haunt us and the progress of our maturation will become more and more delayed and burdened by unfinished business.

For example, the adolescent who is unable to express and fully experience all the tensions and anxieties of his rapidly changing world may well find himself in later life reverting to adolescent patterns of behaviour; or the person who fails adequately to go through the pain of mourning (helped perhaps by too many drugs or the need to keep up a good front) may well find the unresolved, unexpressed grief bursting through in later life in depression, neurosis and so on. I remember a man who failed to mourn his mother's death but carried on in the True Brit tradition, admired by many for his courage and stiff upper lip. A few years later he was made redundant, and this death, the death of his job and the self-esteem that went with it, was the volcano through which all the unresolved agony of his mother's death came pouring, causing a nervous breakdown.

So now we have two anxieties, our finitude and our freedom; the picture is still ambiguous, and already I am trying to think of something to say to make it seem less threatening; there must be an answer. And yet even if I came up with a half-convincing answer, wouldn't that go against all that we have been saying? Life *is* ambiguous, despite anything I might say and despite all our longing for an answer; meaning and meaninglessness are still in conflict, however much we may yearn for the scales to tip in one direction. But if one thing has come out of this search, surely it is the fact of the unique, irreplaceable worth of the human being, the individual value of each person trying to emerge from the stone that imprisons him or her. James Baldwin wrote in *The Fire Next Time*:

> Life is tragic simply because the earth turns and the sun inexorably rises and sets, and one day, for each of us, the sun will go down for the last, last time. Perhaps the whole root of our trouble, the human trouble, is that we will sacrifice all the beauty of our lives, will imprison ourselves in totems, taboos, crosses, blood sacrifices, steeples, mosques, races, armies, flags, nations, in order to deny the fact of death, which is the only fact we have. It seems to me that one ought to rejoice in the *fact* of death – ought to decide, indeed, to *earn* one's death by confronting with passion the conundrum of life. One is responsible to life: it is the small beacon in that terrifying darkness from which we come and to which we shall return. One must negotiate this passage as nobly as possible, for the sake of those who are coming after us. But white Americans do not believe in death, and this is why the darkness of my skin so intimidates them.

I used to find the old saying, 'better to be Socrates and unhappy than a pig and happy', intensely annoying; I was quite sure I'd prefer to be an untroubled pig. But to be a pig, to use all these escape routes we have looked at, is putting off the day of reckoning. Time passes, sooner or later life is going to put in the boot, and what will we have made of this one chance, this one opportunity of life? Saint Exupéry, the French pilot and author, creates the image of the pilot confronting himself and the elements, flying over the quiet houses below, where the people are asleep. This could lead to a sort of 'who dares wins' snobbery, but maybe we have to choose between flying or sleeping. And if we choose to fly, then we have to fly straight into the storm, to confront our anxieties without asking for answers. Keats wrote to his brothers about the one quality which he felt the man of achievement must possess, 'that is, when a man is capable of being in uncertainties, mysteries, doubts, without any irritable searching after fact and reason'. Kierkegaard said that our attitude to anxiety should be like Socrates' calm when facing his execution, as he 'solemnly flourished the cup of poison . . . just as a patient tells the surgeon before a painful operation, "I am ready now." Then anxiety or dread enters and searches every part of his soul, purging it of everything unimportant or worthless, and leading him on his journey.'

In the book of Genesis there is the strange story of Jacob wrestling with a stranger who will not tell him his name. Jacob is alone, separated from family and possessions, and has to fight through the night, even though he is injured. Eventually the stranger says, 'Let me go, for the day is breaking,' but Jacob replies, 'I will not let you go unless you bless me.' The stranger gives Jacob a new name (the symbol of becoming a new self), 'for you have striven with God and with man, and have prevailed.' Our journey is the same: it involves darkness and struggle and the refusal to give in, despite the pain. But it is only by staying true to the conflict and refusing to let go that we reach the daylight and the new birth of ourselves.

We began this chapter by asking where to start the search for meaning, and in looking at man perhaps the answer that we find is that his meaning lies in the search itself. We're not far here from modern psychotherapy, one of whose basic aims is to increase the individual's self-awareness by helping him to clarify inner conflicts which have arisen because he has been forced to block self-awareness at earlier times: he has been unable to move through accumulations of anxiety at various points in his growth, and until he can confront them he will remain unhealed. Freedom is not spontaneous, nor can blocks be lifted magically; the new life involves staying through the night and the struggle. And so with us in our quest for meaning: we have to fight for it. But the fight can be very lonely, because so few are prepared to struggle; instead we put all our energies into filling in the chinks in our armour. Kierkegaard said:

Even if a man is in despair, he can still get on with everyday life . . . he may be praised, looked up to, respected, and pursue all the worldly goals. Worldliness means men just like that, who pawn themselves to the world. They use their gifts, amass money, deal in worldly matters, are shrewd in their calculations, etc., etc. Perhaps they are even mentioned in history, but they are not themselves; in spiritual terms, they have no self, no self for whom they would risk everything, no self before God.

In the eyes of the world it is dangerous to venture, and yet, as Jesus said, 'Whoever cares for his own safety is lost; but if a man will let himself be lost for my sake . . . that man is safe. What does a man gain by winning the whole world at the cost of his true self? What can he give to bring that self back?'

The search for meaning involves the search for one's self. If, in our anxiety at the silent pressures of absurdity and death, we surround ourselves too competently with all the defence mechanisms at our command, then the greatest absurdity of all is that we obliterate the very self we are trying to protect. I remember my fear, when I was working in advertising, that I would die at fifty-four, with two divorces, two Jaguars and a magnificent house in Weybridge, but that as I died I would be asking the agonising question: 'Who am I? What have I done with my time?' Our defences become our enemies. We want to remain children in a reassuring world, but isn't Peter Pan's greatest moment when he actually faces the inevitable and says, 'To die will be an awfully big adventure'? The time we are given is so precious that it seems criminal to waste it, to lose our chance of meaning simply to protect ourselves from fear; can we instead be like Kierkegaard's Socrates, flourish the poisoned goblet of ambiguity and say, 'I am ready now'?

2. 'Is there anybody there?' said the traveller

Our discussion has been fairly bleak so far, rather like the tragedies of Euripides when all the horror has been revealed. It's at that point that Euripides usually wheels on some highly unconvincing god to wind things up neatly, and the resulting strain between the vividly real characters and the formal and unreal deity is a bit like tacking a religious broadcast on to the end of Coronation Street; exit Medea in a chariot drawn by winged dragons, or Annie Walker on a cloud. And I'm equally nervous about introducing God-talk here, because it could so easily degenerate into meaninglessness.

Although 'God' is a word we're all familiar with – and anyone you spoke to would be able to give you a definition of what he or she thinks it means – if we codified all the definitions we would end up with a vast menagerie of different beasts all called God, but no two looking alike. The word 'God' isn't a word you can use like 'chair'; if we talk together about a chair, we both know roughly what the other person means. But if I wander up to someone in the street and say, 'God loves you', I'm liable to open up a world of misunderstanding. For a start, the word 'God' can act like a Masonic handshake: either the other person belongs to the club of believers or he doesn't. If he does believe in whatever he thinks of God as being, then, disregarding the social embarrassment of being accosted by a stranger, we might expect to have a roughly shared language. But if he doesn't believe in 'God', of whatever nature, then it would be just as meaningful for me to have said, 'Prunesquallor loves you' or, 'I feel warmly about humanity.'

But even with a fellow believer, what sort of God am I talking about? When I went to see Monty Python's *Life of Brian* at a cinema in Leicester Square, I had to join a long

queue to get in. A man was standing preaching to the queue
about the need for repentance, belief in God, and so on, and
was being laughed at for his pains. When I came out of the
cinema he was still there. It was raining and he was still
being laughed at. I felt sorry for him and also guilty because
I wasn't at all sure that I would have the courage to do what
he was doing, so I went up to him to wish him well. 'You're
very brave,' I said, pointing at the amused and slightly
hostile queue; 'Ah yes, but the wonderful thing is,' he said,
'that they're all going to *burn*.'

We worship a multitude of different gods from an avenging
burner to Father Christmas; perhaps we must, because to
worship is an intrinsic part of man. Tillich spoke about God
being whatever is a person's ultimate concern – an idea not
far from the origin of the word worship itself, worth-ship:
whatever is of most worth or value to you. The trouble is
that the idols we are given to worship nowadays have very
clay-like feet. What we looked at in the last chapter was the
worship of sex or political systems or new cars and so on,
and we found that such worship was really the product of
man's desire for unity with something greater than himself
or an exercise in papering over the cracks. But the unity was
only temporary, and the cracks had a nasty habit of reap-
pearing. So what about religion? Is this the moment to
produce God like an ace from up the sleeve?

Unfortunately, religion can turn out to be the biggest
cover-up job of them all – the ultimate comfort blanket.
Freud said that you could account for the whole phenomenon of religious experience simply by looking at man's
unconscious mind; you need look no further for the origin of
God or gods than the fact that man is unable to cope with all
the potential disasters and evils of life, and so he invents a
benevolent figure who will probably shield him from harm in
this life and then ensure his personal survival after death,
preferably with lots of bliss thrown in. And this benevolent
figure is none other than a huge blow-up of one's father – the
original Big Daddy. If this is true, then religion must be a
deeply retrogressive force in our lives, something that keeps
us perpetually in a childish state. And there are certainly

various pictures of God which fit this view, whether he is made the rubber stamp of approval for a plush lifestyle, a lucky charm, or the distant monarch on his throne, keeping careful tally of all the good little boys and girls.

Freud's views on religion are an important and helpful warning about the way religion can go off the tracks and become yet another retreat from reality. But they don't tie in very easily with the religion that is a quest for truth nor with the many, many people for whom belief, far from providing an easy ride, brings great hardship, putting them at odds with the state and leading to persecution, labour camps and psychiatric wards. St Paul turned his back on a highly promising career to become a lonely outcast at odds with both Jews and many of his fellow Christians; his search for Christ was no comfort blanket: 'It seems to me God has made us apostles the most abject of mankind. We are like men condemned to death in the arena, a spectacle to the whole universe . . . fools . . . ' And time and again both the people in the Bible and those open enough to let themselves be confronted by it show that, as E.C. Hoskyns wrote, 'To have heard the Bible speak is to be prepared not for maturity, balance, poise, riches, but for the poverty and distress and uncertainty of thought and action that are so desperately characteristic of human life.' Is this the crunch point? Is it that real religion takes humanity, with all the ambiguity and tragedy of life, one hundred per cent seriously, whereas comfort-religion can only go so far before turning its back and saying either, 'I'm all right Jack' or, 'Never mind, it'll all end happily ever after'?

In a way it's like the story of Prometheus, who formed man from clay and then stole fire from heaven to bring him to life; but fire belonged only to the gods, and to punish Prometheus the god Zeus had him chained to a rock where a vulture would gnaw his liver for all eternity. Comfort-religion leaves the fire well alone and lets the gods get on with it – it's best to keep them sweet. It would also prefer people to be chained to rocks rather than make nuisances of themselves; after all, you don't have to take risks or make decisions when you're a clay puppet. How comfortable. How safe. Real religion searches for the fire and seeks to

bring man to life; it would rather risk failure than worship
false gods. Its compassion for humanity involves sacrifice
and total commitment.

But if true religion doesn't worship false gods, what does
it worship? It's at this point that I'd like to abdicate and
bring the chapter to a hurried close, because the answer,
presumably, is 'God', but I'm not at all sure what I mean
when I say that. Braced by my degree in theology, I could, I
think, try to construct some sort of fairly logical model of
what the word God is usually taken to mean, and there are
splendid books which do just that for you. But the trouble is
that the more logical the system, the more well defined the
deity, the less easy I find it to believe in him. In fact, it's
extremely hard to believe in God, this vast, superhuman,
amorphous figure, omnipotent, omniscient, omnipresent;
the longer the definition, the more my heart sinks. I have to
go to the launderette this evening, and very boring it will be,
and I simply can't relate that or indeed many other parts of
my life to this superbeing; what have we in common with
each other? I'm strongly tempted to echo the widow in the
prologue and just say blow the lot of it, but there are
conflicting feelings to deal with. To start with, there's a
feeling of inferiority because I can't believe in what I think I
should believe in; then there's a rebellious feeling of freedom which says, 'Scrap the lot – why waste your time on a
dream?'; and then there's a slightly muddled feeling which
says that perhaps one should dare to say F . . . God to the
old image that seems so irrelevant and yet may be a *sine qua
non* for the mainstream Christian, but that there's something
else as well, less easy to describe or discuss and yet more real
to me as a person, more precious, more full of worth-ship.

But what sort of creature am I finding it so difficult to
believe in? There must be a part of me that still hankers for
the old God who was a being much like us, only a million
times more powerful, and who lived in a definite fixed abode
which I might reach someday: the Greeks – some of them –
would have said on top of Mount Olympus, I used to think
the sky. And if I'm a little schizoid about this God, perhaps
it's because the language of hymns and prayers – the
language of devotion – reinforces the image: every day I

faithfully repeat, 'Our Father, which art in heaven . . .', and I go into a church whose beautiful coloured windows abound with our feathered friends the angels surrounded by artistically placed wisps of cloud. This is the God who must look like Michelangelo's portrayal on the Sistine ceiling: bearded and stern, robed in majesty, liable to speak from the clouds. It is an enormously powerful image and perhaps more tenacious than we'd like to think.

The next version is a less human God. He is still a person, but without a body, and he no longer lives in the sky but somewhere beyond the world, although he keeps it all running and intervenes from time to time. It's here that the problems start because, although you can now counter the funny dig of the Russian cosmonauts – 'We've been up to heaven and there's no one there' – with 'Oh we don't believe in *that* any more, he dwells beyond time and space', it becomes increasingly difficult to understand who or what you're talking about. The mind boggles at trying to take in a consciousness that is disembodied and infinitely extended, capable of seeing and influencing anything at any place or any time or all things in all places at all times . . . And even if you can somehow imagine that, doesn't it leave God as another creature – a billion times more powerful than us, but still a creature capable of being speculated about; something out there, a little like the room in the Kremlin (or the White House) which, presumably, contains the button to finish us all off? I can think about it and try to imagine it, but it still doesn't bear any relation to my life, my pain, my hope.

And perhaps many of us give up the unequal struggle to believe in such a thing, and return gratefully to the wise father figure, the more human figure that we can relate to as a person, even though we have an uneasy feeling that if we think too hard about him he won't be there. But what is our attitude to this person? It's here that we need to remember Freud's warnings, because with a God like this there is going to be a constant danger that we will be acting out of (hidden) self-interest. Take the very act of believing. Pascal said belief could be like placing a bet: if I bet there isn't a God, then if I'm wrong I risk eternal punishment: if I bet there *is* a God, and I'm wrong, then I haven't lost much anyway, but if

I'm right, there's all heaven to win. So it's more sensible to believe and avoid risking hell-fire – and maybe hit the jackpot. Hopefully we have all moved on a bit from Pascal's wager, but there's still a strong risk of us believing because of what we can get out of it.

Looked at in this way, some religion is profoundly immoral. If I do good because I hope God will reward me and I don't do anything bad because God may punish me or because I hope that will cut down my time in purgatory, then I haven't acted in a truly *moral* way at all; I'm just being sensible in the same way that a laboratory rat is sensible when it learns that pushing button 1 means food will come and pushing button 2 means it will get an electric shock. There's no morality in the fact that it soon stops pressing button 2 and sticks to button 1. And if I look to God for reward or punishment, I rob my actions of any moral content – I no longer go round the hospital ward because I think that is something good in itself, but because I hope it will pay dividends; and I don't stop going to massage parlours because I think it is demeaning and depersonalising to both me and the masseuse, but because I'm frightened the eye in the sky will find me out. To believe in God because belief is necessary for salvation robs worship of any sort of moral value; you no longer worship because God is good or right or true but because he's your entry ticket to heaven, and that isn't worship, but common sense – or possibly, low cunning.

If you go on long enough in this vein, God becomes a tyrant whom you're terrified of displeasing and on whom rests your personal survival, so you have got to keep him sweet, and nothing is good or bad in itself but simply a means to an end: heaven or hell. Because it is to do with personal survival, and because it relates to a God 'out there' – something or someone outside the world – worship of this God can be profoundly selfish; the Church becomes a Noah's Ark into which you crawl for safety and then watch everyone else drowning, and your main criterion when you meet someone will be, 'Does he belong – is he one of us?' And if he isn't, then no matter how good or right or true he is, he's still not a member. And because you are in the ark of safety, you are somehow removed from real life, set apart from other people and their concerns, busy with higher things. 'I always look forward to funerals,' the young curate said to me, 'they're such a marvellous opportunity for evangelisation.' In other words, get 'em while they're down. And as people find the traditional God increasingly irrelevant and boring, it is only when they are weak and vulnerable that the Noah's Ark Church is able to pounce. 'Are we to fall upon one or two unhappy people in their weakest moment?' wrote Dietrich Bonhoeffer, 'and force upon them a sort of religious coercion?'

Comfort blanket, moral blackmailer, distant figure in the sky – I hope one learns to reject all these, but I'm still no nearer saying what I *do* believe in, and the grip of the old images is very strong: part of me would love the security of still being able to believe in them. I had dinner once in a Christian commune whose members impressed me by their devotion and simplicity and complete faith – in comparison I felt as faithless and devious as a Borgia in a meadow of spring lambs. They told me that there was always a lot of washing to do so they had prayed to God about it, and a few days later they were given a cheque for enough money to buy a washing machine. During the course of the meal an ominous noise was heard from the scullery, which turned out to be the machine going wrong and overflowing. We all thought about this, and it was decided that maybe the Lord was telling them that they shouldn't have bought the washing machine after all. I felt it would be heretical to suggest a look at the instruction book . . .

There are so many prayer success stories that one hears about, all to do with this benevolent God on tap who seems to be on the end of a private line, but somehow they don't fit in with my experience of life, and I'm tired of feeling guilty and saying that if I believed more strongly I'd see that sort of thing happen too. In fact I've seen the other side of the coin – the bewilderment when tragedy hits a deeply good and believing family and people start saying, 'Why did God allow it? How did he let this happen?', as if there were someone sitting in a heavenly control room, stopping this,

allowing that, presumably according to some deeply laid
plan – although it feels more like whimsy – but capable of
being cajoled if everyone would only pray hard enough. And
as long as the image of the control room is there, worship
will be tinged with self-interest; we shall be siding with
where we think the power is: now, if we could only find the
secret of tapping it effectively . . .

Is this what Bonhoeffer meant when he said, 'We cannot
be honest unless we recognise that we have to live in the
world *etsi deus non daretur* – even if there is no God'
[although God is not a given]? Again, 'God would have us
know that we must live as men who manage our lives
without him.' Because he was executed in a Nazi concentration camp it is impossible for us to know how his thinking
would have developed, but he left behind a tantalising call
for a religionless Christianity, saying that in the modern
world now come of age you no longer need to bring on a
deus ex machina (back to Euripides again!) to provide
answers, explanations or guarantees. Instead, he calls for a
God who, far from being a hypothesis or a sort of appendage
to the world, will grasp men at the centre of their lives. This
means, amongst other things, taking the here and now
seriously; Christianity is concerned with the ultimate, the
last things, but before them come the penultimate, 'the
things before the last', which must be taken just as seriously.

To explain this, Bonhoeffer uses a case very similar to the
one I mentioned in the prologue: 'When I am with someone
who has suffered a bereavement, I often decide to adopt a
"penultimate" attitude . . . remaining silent as a sign that I
share in the bereaved man's helplessness in the face of such a
grievous event, and not speaking the biblical words of
comfort which are, in fact, known to me and available to
me.' There must be a deep concern for the everyday world
of mankind, not the 'transcendental irresponsibility' that
threatens to divert the course of religion. The reason why
you stay silent on funeral visits is that by trying to impose
your own solution you fail to take seriously what the
mourner is going through; there *may* be hope in the future,
but that is not what she can understand *now*. Words of
comfort may make *me* feel better, but they may well prevent

the mourner from being able to give vent to her real feelings.

In Arthur Miller's play *Death of a Salesman* there is a speech that is profoundly religious (religionlessly religious!) in its implications: 'I don't say he's a great man. Willy Loman never made a lot of money. His name was never in the paper. He's not the finest character that ever lived. But he's a human being, and a terrible thing is happening to him. So attention must be paid. He's not to be allowed to fall into his grave like an old dog. Attention, attention must be finally paid to such a person.' The more we lift our eyes to Mount Olympus or devote our attention to looking for a God 'out there', the less attention we pay to the living and the real. If there is a God, and if he is good for anything, then he must turn our eyes away from the sanctuary and the flight of 'the alone to the Alone', push us firmly down the church steps into the crowd outside and, confronting us with humanity, say, 'Attention, attention must be finally paid.'

But even now, I'm still no nearer to saying what I think the word 'God' means, nor is my position so far very different from that of my humanist boss at the magazine. So rather than continuing to speculate about this boring figure in the sky to whom it is so difficult to relate, can we abandon the unequal struggle and say instead that the words, 'I believe in God', are actually shorthand for a whole world of complex ins and outs, perhaps best summed up in two quotations which don't mention the word 'God' at all. The first is from Jung: 'Life is – or has – meaning and meaning-lessness. I cherish the anxious hope that meaning will preponderate and win the battle.' The second is from Dag Hammarskjöld: 'I don't know who – or what – put the question, I don't know when it was put. I don't even remember answering. But at some moment I did answer yes to Someone – or Something – and from that hour I was certain that existence is meaningful and that, therefore, my life, in self-surrender, had a goal.'

The question of God has nothing to do with metaphysical speculation about pie in the sky, but rather comes straight back to our initial questions about meaning or meaningless-ness in existence. You cannot really refer to God as a person or a thing, another being like ourselves, and that is why you

can't really say that God does or doesn't exist; what you can
say, though, is that existence does or does not have meaning. Taking this line of thought further, to say that you
believe in God can mean, effectively, that you believe that
existence is meaningful, or as Schubert Ogden has written,
'The primary use or function of the word "God" is to refer
to the objective ground in reality itself of our ineradicable
confidence in the final worth of our existence.' But as
Hammarskjöld suggests, this is not an armchair theology,
not like sitting at home wondering if the Loch Ness Monster
really exists; it's more like walking by Loch Ness and finding
what looks remarkably like a giant footprint – could it be the
monster, or is it an accident of nature? Whatever it is, it
poses us a question – it is a challenge, a call: after all, if
there's the possibility of a monster in the vicinity, you don't
just sit around and speculate about it.

The path of speculation, our very use of words, is fraught
with dangers. Into the middle of a village, buried deep in the
African jungle, bursts a messenger. He has come from the
next village, three days' journey away, to tell the people that
their country has just been made a British colony and that
they owe allegiance to Queen Victoria. But how to describe
Victoria to people who have never seen a white man, a
wheel, or anything beyond the limits of their patch of jungle
clearing? 'She lives in Buckingham Palace' might become
'she lives in a grass hut taller than a tree'; 'she is very rich
and has a well equipped army' might become 'she has more
bull elephants than the eye can count, and her warriors have
magic spears that speak like thunder and spit fire', and so
on. But suppose we substitute 'God' for Victoria and
ourselves for the natives, won't our language problem be the
same? All we can do is use words and concepts from our own
experience of life to try to picture the unexplainable to
ourselves. So anything we say may possibly point to a truth,
but it won't necessarily be true in itself and it may be
downright misleading.

Paul Tillich said that *any* statement you make about God
is symbolic and cannot be literally true. Indeed the very
word 'God' is a symbol for a reality we can only guess at. We
can say, and perhaps need to say for the sake of our integrity

as human beings, that there is no supreme Being set apart from us, judging, watching and controlling; God is not another person like Queen Victoria. But when we try to say what *is* there, words become misleading and dangerous. Rather than reintroduce a God 'out there' I'd prefer to join the philosophers who say the word 'God' simply stands for those human ideals that command our ultimate devotion. But there's something more – an experience so maddening and elusive that it won't let itself be tied down in words.

If I try to explain what I think is at the root of that experience, it must be with the proviso that words are going to let me down and that, in the end, all I can do is to appeal to our shared experience of life. The experience of finding meaning in existence comes from sensing that we are not isolated individual accidents in the universe, but that all living things share in an ultimate reality – Being itself, the act of being, which is active in every particular being: the absolute, unlimited life force which is in all beings – rather like the breath in the body – the soul. So talk about God is really about Being itself, the act and energy of being, and although Being may have preceded creation and so, in a sense, transcends it, yet it is also in all beings and inseparable from them. You could almost say that it is a shared existence: God and the world, Being and beings, form an organic whole. And so, perhaps, no world – no God. We're not in a position to be able to separate God from the world; in our existence we sense, or fail to sense, a meaning and directedness, Being as pure energy forming all creation, creative Being as the deepest and most real part of what calls us into existence as unique individual human beings. Just as the Africans in the jungle might have struggled to picture Queen Victoria, so our God-talk is an attempt to put that experience into words.

Maybe the time has come to look more closely at such experiences.

The philosopher Wittgenstein (who uttered what should be the epigraph of this chapter – 'Whereof one cannot speak, thereof one must be silent.') spoke about the phenomenon of 'seeing as' – the way we see or interpret facts in a special way. He used the old idea of puzzle pictures: at first

all you see is a page covered with dots but then, after looking
at it for a time, instead of seeing a random collection of dots
you see that they form the picture of a man. Belief in God,
the experience of faith, is when the very random dots that go
to make up one's life suddenly seem to take on a pattern or
purpose.

So perhaps the task of religion is to open our eyes, to help
us to see more clearly, not to shove a foregone conclusion
down our obedient throats. Almost all the forms of behaviour that we looked at in the last chapter tended to act
like blinkers in people's lives, preventing them from looking
up and seeing where they were, the real pattern of their
lives. Often the most helpful reply one could give from the
problem page was a simple restatement of people's problems
and their position in more ordered terms so that they could
stop and see; in counselling, too, often the most helpful
thing you can do is to provide space and time for the other
person just to stop and see where they are. The rush of life,
all the business of making a living or trying to find a job,
keeping a roof over one's head, looking after the family, all
this can keep our eyes firmly fixed on the ground. As
Wordsworth said:

> The world is too much with us; late and soon,
> Getting and spending, we lay waste our powers.

Or T.S. Eliot, more cynically, 'I have measured out my life
with coffee spoons.' It is perhaps in this condition that, as
Jesus said, 'They may look and look, but see nothing; they
may hear and hear, but understand nothing.' The effect of
all this rushing, and the need for stillness, are well understood by a character in Ursula Le Guin's book *The Farthest
Shore*:

> Try to choose carefully, Arren, when the great choices
> must be made. When I was young I had to choose between
> the life of being and the life of doing. And I leapt at the
> latter like a trout to a fly. But each deed you do, each act,
> binds you to itself and to its consequences, and makes you
> act again and yet again. Then very seldom do you come
> upon a space, a time like this, between act and act, when

you may stop and simply be. Or wonder who, after all, you are.

Is that what prayer is about? Perhaps the moment has come to look more closely at the dots that make up the picture, and to see if any kind of pattern emerges. But I can only say where I think *I* see a pattern emerging – to anyone else it may still just look like a blur of dots; like a puzzle picture, life is ambiguous. With the dying Rabelais maybe the most we can say is, 'I go to seek a great perhaps.' But the search for the great perhaps needs to start first of all with the question of man. In the last chapter I proposed the possibility that man is a freak, an overgrown ape, an accident of evolution. But we can't be certain about that, just as we can't be certain where man is going. Was Nietzsche right when he said, 'Man is a rope stretched between beast and superman . . . man is great, in that he is a bridge and not a goal. Man can be loved, in that he is a transition and a perishing.' It seemed inadequate for man to define himself in terms of society or possessions or even his own self-development; the nature of man is dynamic, unfinished, and he is also capable of losing his humanity and almost rejoining the animals.

So where is man headed? In a sense, to ask questions about the nature of man is also to ask questions about meaning; to ask, 'What am I here for?', to look at life and one's experience of humanity may lead to saying, 'It's all a sick joke' – Rabelais' other reported dying words were, 'Bring down the curtain, the farce is over' – or may lead one towards God-talk. In this case to say 'I believe in God' would, when unscrambled, mean that I don't think my life feels like an accident in the universe, and that in my life and my experience of other people I have sensed that behind human life there is a power which is most fully expressed in the human personality and which is utterly trustworthy.

I remember visiting an atheist friend the day after her father died. She was terribly upset, of course, but she was also strangely stern – 'I cannot believe that the personality I knew and loved in all its richness, has simply come to an end.' When you love friends, family, husband, wife, lover, children, and when you have the privilege of being with a personality that gradually unfolds itself to you in all its infinite complexity and richness (and annoyingness!) and you become aware of all the unfathomed depths of emotion, personality, wisdom and spirit, then it becomes increasingly hard to see this human being as an accident of evolution.

But this doesn't just apply to people you love. I once worked with a rather pompous, overbearing man who really used to get up my nose. He fell ill, and was found to be dying of cancer. During the few remaining weeks of his life I was able to spend a lot of time with him. Perhaps I should say that I was *privileged* to be able to spend time with him, because what I saw was an almost miraculous transformation; in inverse proportion to the withering of his body and the shrinking of this big, burly man to a haggard cripple, I witnessed the flowering of his personality and in particular his courage in the face of excruciating pain, and his tremendous honesty as he faced all the conflicting emotions of waiting for death. In a strange way, during the time we spent together, as I watched his physical torture but also the flowering of the riches of his spirit, I grew to love this man I had been unable to like. I cannot believe that such courage and honesty, such human warmth and love that seemed to burst out of him, were just an accident, here today, gone tomorrow and in the final analysis irrelevant. On the contrary, it was as if his very being was reaching out and finding its meaning for the first time.

Faced with such beauty of the human spirit one feels a deep sadness; it is always possible that the spirit has grown despite everything, and that life is still basically absurd and meaningless – 'The days of man are but as grass: he flourishes as a flower of the field; when the wind goes over it, it is gone: and its place will know it no more' (Psalm 103). Hence the famous lines in Virgil's *Aeneid*, when Aeneas sees the painting of the battles of the Trojan War, showing his dead comrades and all the acts of bravery and sorrow; he cries and says, '*Sunt lacrimae rerum et mentem mortalia tangunt*' – literally, 'Here are tears of things and the affairs of mortal man touch the heart.' The 'tears of things' apply to all the ventures of the human spirit if taken in the context of man's mortality.

In Peter Shaffer's play *The Royal Hunt of the Sun*, the conquistador Pizarro sees time as a greater enemy than the Incas; in the light of death, the mighty empire of Peru and Pizarro's own victories are meaningless. Having achieved the seemingly impossible conquest, he confides to his captive, Atahualpa, the Sovereign Inca:

> I'm going to die! And the thought of that dark has for years rotted everything for me, all simple joy in life . . . That prison the priest calls Sin Original, I know as Time. And seen in time everything is trivial. Pain. Good. God is trivial in that seeing. Trapped in this cage we cry out, 'There's a gaoler; there must be. At the last, last, last of lasts he will let us out. He will! He will! . . .' But, oh my boy, no one will come for all our crying.

And yet, despite his distress at being confronted again with the whole tragedy of the Trojan War, 'For the first time Aeneas' fears were allayed, and for the first time he dared to hope for life', and Peter Shaffer in his introduction to the *Royal Hunt of the Sun* says:

> Pizarro recovers the savour [the essential joy in man] a little, a very little. For once, as a man, he holds on (and here is a faith, for the facts counsel against it) out of deep, 'useless', barely acknowledged affection, to the life thread of another man. He celebrates in his stubbornness the wonder of a life. He is left with no answers, ultimately with no existence. But in no very paradoxical sense he recovers joy, by finding real grief. The frost melts. As Genet said: 'To see the soul of a man is to be blinded by the sun.'

A few times in our lives we are privileged to be blinded by that sun. I find it hard to believe such light can be put out, that it is not here for a reason.

Another ambiguity is the context in which man is set. Why is there a world at all, rather than nothing, and why is it an ordered world rather than chaos? This isn't just the question of 'Who set up the big bang?' or why there was a big bang at all, but is also to do with the feeling expressed by the astronomer Sir James Jeans, 'The universe shows evidence of a designing or controlling power that has . . . the tendency to think in the way which, for want of a better word, we describe as mathematical . . . The universe begins to look more like a great thought than a great machine.' In other words, perhaps rationality is at least as good an answer to the riddle of the universe as is chance. But the universe and creation, Einstein's God who is 'subtle but not malicious', are too far from my own experience really to speak to me.

Closer to home is the experience of nature. Perhaps it is risky to try to build an argument on something so personal, but the fact remains that sometimes in nature I feel confronted by something other than my own subjective emotions, something which addresses me and takes or forces me out of myself. There is something in nature which suggests a reality that we have lost touch with in the cities – a presence, a challenge, a promise – something above and beyond the little kingdom of our individual minds. Wordsworth became a sort of guru at Grasmere, visited by people from all over Europe (even though he was so disappointing in the flesh) because of his awareness of this presence:

> I have learned
> To look on nature, not as in the hour
> Of thoughtless youth; but hearing often-times
> The still, sad music of humanity,
> Nor harsh nor grating, though of ample power
> To chasten and subdue. And I have felt
> A presence that disturbs me with the joy
> Of elevated thoughts; a sense sublime
> Of something far more deeply interfused,
> Whose dwelling is the light of setting suns,
> And the round ocean and the living air,
> And the blue sky, and in the mind of man.

Iris Murdoch writes about the experience of seeing a kestrel:

> I am looking out of my window in an anxious and resentful state of mind, oblivious of my surroundings, brooding perhaps on some damage done to my prestige. Then

suddenly I observe a hovering kestrel. In a moment everything is altered. The brooding self with its hurt vanity has disappeared. There is nothing now but kestrel. And when I return to thinking of the other matter it seems less important. And of course this is something which we may also do deliberately: give attention to nature in order to clear our minds of selfish care.

A sunset, a seashore, a rose – if we are only open enough, something speaks to us through nature. Gerard Manley Hopkins had no doubt whose voice it is:

> The world is changed with the grandeur of God.
> It will flame out, like shining from shook foil.

People don't see it, he says, because of the grind of everyday existence – 'Generations have trod, have trod, have trod.'

> And for all this, nature is never spent;
> There lives the dearest freshness deep down things;
> And though the last lights off the black West went
> Oh, morning, at the brown brink eastward, springs -
> Because the Holy Ghost over the bent
> World broods with warm breast and with ah! bright
> wings.

A nun once told me that just walking in the country can be a meditation; walking slowly, open to the sounds and sights around you, stopping to look at a cobweb covered with dew or to listen to a stream. There is the 'dearest freshness' there, if we only had the time to get out of our cars and wait for it to speak to us.

The sense of 'the other', of being addressed by something outside oneself, can also be vividly present in great art. Although the *Mona Lisa* is actually boxed in, roped off and guarded to protect her from possible vandals amongst the crowds of tourists, I had the strange fantasy that she was really glassed in and caged to protect the tourists from her: from their being unsettled by that unearthly smile. Or think of the effect of hearing the 'Liebestod' from Wagner's *Tristan und Isolde*, as the love theme contorts and develops and grows in painful intensity until it finally resolves on a tonic chord: for a moment you are forced into stillness as the deep yearning is transformed into fulfilment. Our reaction to art, what moves, uplifts or disturbs us, is so personal, but surely our basic reaction is not far from that of Dora in Iris Murdoch's novel *The Bell*, as she looks at a Gainsborough in the National Gallery:

> . . . here at last was something real and something perfect . . . something which her consciousness could not wretchedly devour, and by making it part of her fantasy make it worthless . . . The pictures were something real outside herself, which spoke to her in kindly and yet in sovereign tones . . . she felt that she had had a revelation . . . she gave a last look at the painting, still smiling, as one might smile in a temple, favoured, encouraged, and loved . . . she remembered that she had been wondering what to do; but now, without her thinking about it, it had become obvious. She must go back to Imber at once. Her real life, her real problems, were at Imber; and since, somewhere, something good existed, it might be that her problems would be solved after all. There was a connection; obscurely she felt, without yet understanding it, she must hang onto that idea: there was a connection.

In Peter Shaffer's play *Amadeus*, the composer Salieri describes his anguish on hearing Mozart's music: 'What is this *pain*? What is this *need* in the sound? Forever unfulfillable, yet fulfilling him who hears it utterly . . . I was suddenly frightened. It seemed to me I had heard a voice of God.' Mankind's sense of longing, as expressed in great art, can be deeply tragic in the context of *lacrimae rerum*, of man's finitude and mortality. But it can also act as a pointer, seeming to direct us to something beyond itself or as if something else is speaking through it. As with humanity, as with creation, so with art, we feel ourselves confronted by 'the other'.

There is another way in which we are confronted by something outside ourselves, and which is perhaps less personalistic than our reactions to art and nature: this is the voice of moral demand in our lives. You can explain away a lot of morality in terms of social and cultural conditioning, or Freud's super-ego – a kind of built-in parent – but I'm not sure that this explains why man is a moral being in the first place or why there is an absolute moral demand which goes beyond the relative and may lead a man to reject familial or social pressures. This is the sort of demand that confronted some of the Old Testament prophets, often to their dismay and personal danger. It forced them to go against the whole religious establishment and all the accepted ideas of God's dealings with Israel and to say, 'Don't just sit on your backsides all confident that God's on your side and will look after you; because you've got it terribly wrong and now you're going to have to pay the price.' It's hard to believe that the moral imperatives that drove men like Amos and Jeremiah, or that set a man like Dietrich Bonhoeffer on the road that led to his murder in a concentration camp, just came out of thin air. In a sense, the whole of the previous chapter had a moral undercurrent because it was to do with being human, and man is a moral being who needs to ask, 'What ought I to be in the process of becoming?' All the unsatisfactory roads we looked at seemed to run away from the demands of personal responsibility.

But where does the call of personal responsibility come from, if it is just something conditioned into us by society or culture or parents, just something that man had to learn in order to survive in a group? Where does this force come from, that may set us against all we know and make us seek a totally new path, break new ground? This is perhaps where Matthew Arnold's definition of God fits in. He spoke of 'the enduring power, not ourselves, which makes for righteousness'. Here again, it is the sense of 'the other', of something outside oneself; and here again, the picture is ambiguous – the pattern *I* think I can see made by the dots may be completely meaningless to the next man.

One last area of life which seems to point to 'the other' but which again is highly personal, is the experience of man's undefined longing, restlessness, the feeling of being on a quest. This is something which either makes sense to you or doesn't, in much the same way that Don Quixote is either a silly old fool or something greater – a visionary and dreamer.

But how to describe this longing when it hides itself in so
many ways and the force behind it is diverted into other
channels? You have only to go into the singles or gay bars to
see something of its effect: the hungry, hopeful eyes that
watch the door each time it opens, thinking that perhaps this
time, here will be the one . . . This longing can be reduced to
a mere exchange of sex, a different girl/boy every night, but
the ruthlessness with which it is pursued perhaps shows some
of the desperation and emotional force behind it. I once read
somewhere that the worst feeling in the world is the home-
sickness that comes over a man occasionally when he is at
home.

In his autobiography Bertrand Russell wrote:

> The centre of me is always and eternally a terrible pain – a
> curious wild pain – a searching for something beyond what
> the world contains, something transfigured and infinite –
> the beatific vision – God – I do not find it, I do not think it
> is to be found – but the love of it is my life – it's like
> passionate love for a ghost. At times it fills me with rage,
> at times with wild despair, it is the source of gentleness
> and cruelty and work, it fills every passion that I have – it
> is the actual spring of life within me. I can't explain it or
> make it seem anything but foolishness – but whether
> foolish or not, it is the source of whatever is any good in
> me.

Is such pain ultimately tragic, because it stems from man's
restless spirit, isolated and afraid in an alien universe,
longing to return to the womb? Or is it a pointer to another
level of reality beyond what we can apprehend: a reality
which needs to be taken into account if we are to achieve
wholeness of vision? Because we don't understand what it is
we're longing for, the search takes us down blind alley after
blind alley, making us pursue love or sex or success or fame
or money or whatever; and yet even when we finally reach
our goal it still isn't enough. Perhaps the closest one can get
to peace is in the experience of love, of knowing and being
known, of accepting and being accepted, of being taken out
of oneself by someone whose reality is just as substantial as
one's own, whose safety and happiness are just as or even

more important. Yet in the end I am not sure that another human being can ever quite staunch the sense of longing that comes from our deep aloneness, our quest for meaning.

Nor does society seem to have the answer. I don't want to return to gloom and despondency, but what sort of experience of meaninglessness and unfulfilled longing, unanswerable by any man-made society, can have led to the crisis of alcoholism in Russia, or to a rate of suicide amongst adolescents in the USA that makes it the third highest cause of death after accidents and homicide? More youngsters die by their own hand than from all the infectious diseases or diabetes or appendicitis or what-have-you put together. In Britain, suicide has become the second most common cause of death amongst the young, and nearly a quarter of all acute medical beds are occupied by overdose victims. In northeast Wiltshire, the first part of Britain to start child-maltreatment registers, analysis of 147 families known to have suffered child neglect or abuse over two generations showed that of 560 children born over twenty-one years, 513 had been neglected, assaulted or both, and forty-one had *died*, possibly at their parents' hands. In 1979 the National Health Service issued over forty-one million prescriptions for sedatives, hypnotics and tranquillisers. A survey of 1966 showed that 7 per cent of men and 13 per cent of women suffered from depression. A 1978 survey of a working-class London area showed serious depression in one out of every three women surveyed. These facts, taken at random from medical journals, do seem to point to a crisis of meaning: would people suffer so much if they could see a meaning or purpose to their lives? Jung said, 'A psychoneurosis must be understood, ultimately, as the suffering of a soul which has not discovered its meaning.' But is there an ultimate meaning, or can we only find our meaning' try to satisfy our longing, in the transitory things of life?

These are the sort of dots that go to make up my puzzle picture. I wouldn't really care if God existed or not if it meant having to relate my life to, and speculate about, some alien puppet-master. What I do care about, passionately, is whether Being itself has meaning, can be trusted. We looked

at the experience of being confronted by something or
someone other than oneself – a kestrel, a picture, a person.
In the same way, existence itself confronts us and it is
possible to feel that life is a responsibility or challenge laid
on us, and yet in which we are supported and sustained.
Obviously this is much vaguer than traditional God-
language, but what I'm trying to get across is the idea, not so
much of a being who may or may not exist and who is
anyway over there somewhere, but rather an idea concerning existence itself – that there is an undergirding reality
more substantial than anything we can know or understand,
a reality that brings into being all that exists and may be
sensed in all that exists, a reality that sustains us and yet
which challenges. God, for want of another word, is within
me, the reason I exist; God holds me in being and calls me
into newness of being. Beyond that, beyond my basic trust in
Being, I'm not sure that I want to go. Looking at the puzzle
picture, I have chosen to interpret it in a certain way: I
cannot prove the meaning or meaninglessness of my life one
way or the other; I can only choose to interpret it in the light
of areas of experience that I find particularly meaningful and
which seem to me to hold pointers to a reality above and
beyond what I can see or understand – what has been called,
living life 'on the evidence of its highest moments'. As R.D.
Laing has said, 'Those who hear melodies do not have to
prove that melodies exist because some people who do not
hear them say they do not.'

It is possible that this talk of puzzle pictures, and of trying
to dispense with the idea of God as a person or a being, is
profoundly irritating or upsetting. Knowledge is power, a
way of possessing something, and to the Western mind
knowledge has got to be very factual and logical – a chair is a
chair, a chair is not a table, I know that there is a chair in the
middle of the room. We can have the same attitude to God:
there is a God, he is X, Y and Z, I can be absolutely certain
about this and want everyone else to be certain too. The
danger of this approach is that it makes belief in God the
primary religious function. And perhaps that's the most
common definition of religion – 'Oh, it means belief in God';
if you are a believer you try to find ways to maintain, protect

or strengthen that belief and, if you are a non-believer, you just get on with the job of living or perhaps cast wistful glances at your believing friends; or else you try to find solid arguments to demolish this retrograde superstition.

But I'm not sure that thought and knowledge, belief *in* something, is the primary religious function. I'm usually unimpressed by the people who say proudly, 'Oh, I've never had a day's doubt in my life', because they feel cold – they *are* cold: they've got their treasure safely under lock and key. The people who impress are the ones who don't make a song and dance about their belief in God, but who get on with the business of trying to *live* God; for them it's not a matter of right thoughts but of right actions. Perhaps the primary religious function is how one chooses to live one's life.

A good illustration of this distinction can be found in the story of God's revelation to Moses in the burning bush. Moses says that the Hebrews won't believe God has sent him unless he can tell them God's name. (To know someone's name is to have power over them; it means that they are a thing or a being, something definable.) God's answer is that his name is 'I am who I am' or simply 'I am'. This could mean any one of a hundred things – 'I am becoming who I am becoming' or 'I let be what I let be', because the Hebrew word 'to be' is a dynamic one that includes the ideas of causing and becoming. The one thing it is *not* is static; in other words, God's name cannot be said to describe something which just is, rather is it a description of pure act and energy. He is Being itself which lets be, which brings everything that is into existence. Another understanding of the name would be 'my name is nameless'; this is in line with the commandments not to make any image of God and not to pronounce his name in vain, that is to say, it frees man from making an idol of God, from the idea that he is a father, a person, a being like ourselves. In other words, God refuses to give Moses any easy answers or clear-cut definitions. He doesn't send him back to the Hebrews saying, 'Hey guys, God is X, Y and Z and we've got to believe in him.' Instead he has to go back saying, 'A power I cannot define or understand or see has set me a task and given me a promise.'

This approach leads us to the ancient Christian tradition that the only thing you can say about God is what he is *not*. 'The true vision and the true knowledge of what we seek,' said St Gregory of Nyssa, 'consists precisely in not seeing, in an awareness that our goal transcends all knowledge and is everywhere cut off from us by the darkness of incomprehensibility.' Early theologians, forced into trying to define the indefinable, felt the truth of this. Hilary of Poitiers said:

> The errors of heretics and blasphemers force us to deal with unlawful matters, to scale perilous heights, to speak unutterable words, to trespass on forbidden ground. Faith ought in silence to fulfil the commandment, worshipping the Father, reverencing with him the Son, abounding in the Holy Spirit. The error of others compels us to err in daring to embody in human terms truths which ought to be hidden in the silent veneration of the heart.

And talking about the Trinity, St Augustine wrote that 'human language labours altogether under great poverty of speech'. But he feels that he has to give a definition, 'not that it might be spoken but that it might not be left unspoken'.

If the religious attitude, rather than being belief in something, is an attitude of acceptance and openness to being, like Dag Hammerskjöld answering 'yes' to life, finding existence meaningful 'and that . . . [my] life, in self-surrender, had a goal', then the path of 'unknowing' may be the only answer. In fact it can come as a blessed relief after struggling to make yourself believe in what you feel you *ought* to believe, to accept that what is asked of you is not to do an exam paper called 'six impossible things you must believe before breakfast', but simply to get on with the business of living the life of self-giving love. And perhaps many Christians today would feel a lot easier if they were able to make the painful step of abandoning the quest for certainty – is it that need for certainty that keeps so many of us so painfully immature? – and move on to the path of accptance: accepting life's ambiguity, accepting the darkness that surrounds God, or meaning, or Being.

The great fourteenth-century spiritual classic, *The Cloud*

of Unknowing, has so much to say to the modern Christian because so many of us find ourselves in that cloud; instead of getting on with a life of prayer and love we keep trying to struggle our way out of the darkness, demanding certainty and answers. Instead of living God, we just *think* God. Stop struggling, says the author of *The Cloud*, 'because he may well be loved, but not thought. By love he may be caught and held, but by thinking never. Strike that thick cloud of unknowing with the sharp dart of longing love, and on no account whatever think of giving up.'

No, the Christian does not have easy answers. Yes, life is ambiguous and the conflict of meaning and meaninglessness still confronts us. Perhaps this chapter has been saying that, as we dig down to the roots of the dilemma, we are given clues or hints as to the answer; but they are clues, not proofs, and we are left to make of them what we will. If nothing else, we can learn to trust the struggle itself, learn to be still and to listen, learn to dwell in the cloud of unknowing; the cloud which, traditionally, is the very seat of God's glory and whose darkness we can trust because, as Henry Vaughan said:

> There is in God, some say,
> A deep but dazzling darkness . . .

When I use the word 'God' again in this book, when I refer to that 'deep but dazzling darkness', the temptation for both me and the reader may be to revert to the old familiar images and the sense of security they bring. Can we instead bear in mind that I'll be trying to use the word as shorthand or as a symbol for something far more complex and mysterious – the sort of experience hinted at by Jung and Hammarskjöld – to do with the sense of call and grace, and the gut feeling that behind everything is a reality which, although we can only guess at it, is completely to be trusted. When I use the word 'God', it will not be the simple name of a known quantity; it will be the symbol of the uncertainty and hope, the *experience* that this chapter has been trying to point to: the sense that we belong.

3 Jesus – question or answer

In Chaucer's *Troilus and Criseyde* there's a moment when Troilus and Pandarus are together keeping watch for Cressida. 'Oh there she is, I can see her in the distance, how beautiful, how wonderful,' says Troilus (or words to that effect). 'Don't be stupid,' says Pandarus, 'that's just a cart full of manure.' If this were a book about science and I asserted as a fact that if you drop a lead weight it will float to the ceiling, I suppose someone might believe me (it's amazing what authority the printed word can have), but even a three-year-old would only need to pick up a heavy object and drop it to be able to say, 'Cobblers'. If this were a book about any of the arts, I could say, 'Donatello's *St George* is the greatest sculpture in the world,' or, 'Ronald Colman's best movie was *Random Harvest*', and although you might disagree with me (stand up the person who said, 'Who's Ronald Colman?'), we would at least be able to compare views in front of a movie screen or in the Bargello in Florence. Or if this were a book about morality, I could quote statistics about prostitution in Victorian London and say why I don't think it's immoral to be a prostitute if your only other option is to starve. And presumably we could both verify the statistics, even if we didn't agree about the conclusions I'd drawn from them.

Unfortunately, this is a book about religion, which means that it is trying to deal with areas of life which you can't test in the laboratory, or sit and watch, or draw up statistics and sets of rules about, and yet which are supposed to be real. In our late-twentieth-century way, which is really as old as Aristotelian logic, we tend to say, 'If it's real, prove it.' So after the last chapter I feel very aware that where I was saying, 'Look, I think I can see Cressida there', anyone else might say, 'Don't be a prat, that's just a load of manure' (or

62

something less polite).

Although I'm as much a product of the 'if it's real, prove it' school as anyone else, I'm not sure that I can apply anything so simple to the complexities of life as I experience it, not would books on science, the arts or morality be quite as simple to write as I may have suggested. To take science as an example, probably most of us who are of an unscientific bent of mind imagine that the world still goes on according to Newtonian principles; you can define reality in terms of mass, position and velocity, and the physical world is composed of fundamental, indivisible atoms of specifiable mass which obey certain general laws of motion and mechanics. To look at modern science and quantum mechanics is to have this rug of certainty pulled out from under your feet: nothing is simple, and the old Meccano universe is replaced by fields of energy and sequences of vibratory patterns. The electron, depending on the way it is observed, behaves *either* as a wave *or* as a particle; both are valid, but observation of the electron as a wave rules out observation of it as a particle.

Dr Robert Oppenheimer speaks of a 'duality' that applies to the nature of light and of all matter. Meantime, scientists enter a mysterious world of hypothesis and conjecture: because I believe such and such to be true, then so and so must exist, so I must find ways of proving that it exists or ways of proving that it does not exist. So Einstein wrote, 'A theory can be proved by experiment, but no path leads from experiment to the birth of a theory.' Hence quarks, neutrinos and the like, where you may be dealing with particles of zero mass, electrically neutral, and no one knows which particles are truly elementary (that is, can't be reduced to anything smaller) and which are simply different states of the same particle; and there are some of which, although we *believe* they are there, no one has yet been able to prove the existence. Underneath the world of common sense, which seems so lucid and Newtonian to us, is a more mysterious reality which reveals itself to the mind in many different ways, according to the way it is approached. No longer can we think of immutable Laws of Nature just waiting to be revealed like the mechanism of a clock when it is opened

(with God flitting around like 'the ghost in the machine').
Instead, as Heisenberg has pointed out, science has moved
from being an objective observer to being an actor in the
interplay between man and nature.

And what would I be describing if I wrote about art?
Would I give a chemical analysis of the blobs of paint on a
canvas, or talk about how all the figures in Caravaggio's
Deposition from the Cross radiate like spokes of a wheel
from the axis of Nicodemus' knee? All this might be helpful
– and it takes time and commitment, perhaps, to learn how
to encounter a work of art – but whether or not I know about
Caravaggio, about chiaroscuro, perspective, and so forth,
the fact remains that a fine picture is not just the sum of all
that has gone to make it up: there is something more – there
is communication, something highly personal, something
almost impossible to describe in words. And it is the same
with morality or statistics. In the end they are dealing with
human beings, and the human personality is something you
simply cannot quantify. I could draw up a list of all the
factors that go to make up the person I love – chemical,
socio-economic, psychological, sociological, and so on – and
although that might help to increase my understanding, yet
the whole realm of what goes on between us would be
relatively untouched, and to me that world, although almost
impossible to describe or share, is the most real and the most
important.

So perhaps the religious assertion that there is an underlying depth to reality, something more than just the nuts and
bolts of existence, isn't too far removed from our experience
of life. Of course, if you now turn round and say art is a load
of rubbish and people are just victims of pre-determined
patterns, then there isn't much more to say. Life preserves
its ambiguous face, but I hope that at least I've shown there
are two sides to the story, whichever one may choose to
believe. I hope I've suggested, too, that life is all the poorer
if you are not aware of the many different levels of reality,
and perhaps that the most precious levels of our existence
are precisely those that defy definition and refuse to fit into
the categories of 'if it's real, prove it'. I'm not trying to sneak
God in through the back door here, but simply saying that

there are heights and depths of living that can't be fitted into
the narrow vision of the purely practical, and that for some
of us these experiences are more easily explained in terms of
the 'holy' in being, the 'and more' in reality, than just by
chance. Rather than climbing back onto the old treadmill of
trying to argue the existence of God from the evidence of
nature and so on, I'm talking about something much more
immediate, something we can all experience – the sense of
presence, mystery or power coming through nature, people
or great art.

One of the holiest places I've ever seen is the shrine of the
Delphic oracle. Set high up in the hills near Athens, it was
one of the most sacred places of ancient Greece. When I was
there, it was crammed with sweating Dutch tourists and
yelling street photographers, and yet its stillness was untouched. A Roman who visited the shrine reported that the
motto of the Delphic oracle was *Vocatus atque non vocatus
Deus aderit* – 'Whether he is called or not, the god will
come.' And that is indeed the feeling you get there. This
sense of the holy has been described as *mysterium
tremendum et fascinans*, which encapsulates much of what
we have been saying. *Mysterium* means something transcending human intelligence, a secret thing that keeps its
mystery, that defies categorisation, that emits a sense of the
numinous – 'There is something/someone more here than I
can understand.' *Tremendum* means, literally, something to
be trembled at, hence fearful, formidable, tremendous. It
points to the otherness of what it is we have encountered,
something more than our finite, created being; something
transcendent. *Fascinans* means enchanting, fascinating –
perhaps a word too close to witchcraft for our liking, but in
this context meaning something warm that draws us to itself,
unveils itself to us, gives us grace.

In other words, we have a dual reaction of drawing back
and drawing near, just as what we encounter has a dual
reality, that of time and of the finite, and yet also something
more than that. Something too that reveals itself not in a
special, unique way, just for me, but in the same way for
everybody. But the Dutch tourists sweated and photo-
graphed and chatted their way over the site of Delphi and

then went off for a good lunch in a local restaurant. I felt, maybe mistakenly, that they hadn't really taken it in at all. In the same place, at the same time, looking at the same things, I felt awed by the *mysterium tremendum et fascinans*, and I felt that they did not experience a similar awe. But who was right?

If I had been an ancient Greek visiting Delphi in a thunderstorm, I might have taken that experience of awe as a sort of blueprint to help me understand the deepest nature of reality: there are supernatural forces at work in the world, that throw thunderbolts, and need to be appeased. You might find a particular experience in your life so impressive that it would serve as a focus for understanding the whole riddle of your existence love or hate or war or harmony or – Marxist theory. To be a Christian is to take Christ as the blueprint, the clue to the mystery. But clues aren't direct answers. They can be ambiguous and puzzling. If you grapple with them for long enough they will tell you where to look, but sometimes, if you take them too literally, they can send you astray.

A friend of mine was interrogated for several days by the police of an iron-curtain country. He was not tortured, but he was deprived of sleep and subjected to relays of questioners, often working the old soft/hard technique. He was frightened, of course, especially by the 'hard' interrogators, but the most frightening figure was a man he never met face to face, a man who stayed in the shadows, who came and went, and to whom all the others seemed to defer. My friend began to feel that the conflict was with this man, even though he never saw him clearly; he was the source of the questions and determined the pattern the interrogation would follow; it was possible to guess at the way his mind was moving through the actions of his subordinates, but it was impossible to be sure because the figure remained concealed in the background – there was no direct contact.

If we search for the historical Jesus, our problem is much the same; we have only the voices of others to go on, others who came from an alien culture and thought-world, who wrote with specific ends in view and whom we are unable to question – it is they who question us. And behind them lurks

the figure who is confronting us. If we look to living
witnesses, who are we going to believe? Is it the same Jesus
who is adored by the Dutch Reformed Church supporters of
apartheid in South Africa, by the segregated churches in the
Deep South of the USA, by the drive-in, Cadillac-filled
extravaganza churches, by the extreme Protestant church in
Ulster, by the 'Moonies', by the people who organise
endless jumble sales, by the nuns working in the Calcutta
slums, by the priest holding the hand of a dying man? Who
are we to believe? Perhaps Christianity is the great mystery
religion – it has more creeds and heads than the Hydra. We
must tread carefully, and take the witnesses as we find them.

   But who are the original witnesses? All we have to go on
are the four ancient books called gospels, whose authors we
can only guess at, and whose purposes are unclear. There
has been a sort of conspiracy of silence in the Church about
the extent to which modern critical study of the New
Testament calls into question much of the Christian story as
received at Sunday School or at one's mother's knee.
Perhaps some churches keep their congregations up to date,
but on the whole there seems to be a deceitful gap between
what the clergy have picked up of modern studies and what
they are prepared to let their congregations know. Typically,
we are supposed to believe that the gospels are like straight
history books or biographies: Jesus did this, that and the
other, and you either believe it or you don't.

   The history approach is tempting but has problems. Even
with recent history it can be impossible to discover the
objective truth of an event. You have only to look at the
memoirs and reminiscences of those serving in the Wilson
government, for example, to see flat contradictions between
the different accounts. It would be easy to say cynically, 'Oh,
well, politicians never tell the truth anyway', but it is more
likely that each person wrote down what he or she saw as the
truth and that each saw something different; we may never
know the objective truth. The same thing applies to conversations, which can work on at least three levels: what I
think I am saying: what it is I am *actually* saying: what *you*
think I am saying. Studies of counselling and of chair-
manship have shown how vital it is for both parties in a

dialogue to be absolutely clear about what is *actually* being said – but how often does this happen in our lives? And do we see what is actually happening, or do our emotions, preconceptions and so on colour our response?

I had to take a memorial service which was attended by the local Tory MP. Afterwards, a socialist friend told me how furious he was at the man's impudence and pomposity in marching loudly down the aisle during the prayers, making sure he was seen by everyone. Another (Tory) friend told me that the MP had slipped into his place quietly and discreetly so as not to disturb anyone. Both my witnesses were people I trust, both had seen exactly the same event take place, but the accounts are completely contradictory. What really happened? Sometimes it is difficult for us to distinguish between what is real and what we would like to believe is real. Clark Gable died after filming *The Misfits*. 'Like a gentleman he made his last shot and then died a day later,' said John Huston, the film's director. Actually, Gable died some weeks later, but it would have been true to the man to have died as Huston suggested.

But suppose my witnesses come from a totally alien culture with different thought-worlds and philosophies, how much more confused the picture becomes. I asked an American Indian what the symbol of a dark cloud stood for; to my eyes it seemed threatening and ominous. He replied that it stood for good luck and hope for the future. A snake meant wisdom and bravery, in me it triggered disgust. Similarly, the authors of the gospels were writing in a cultural environment we can only guess at, just as we can only guess at their motives. It seems likely that they wrote within the context of groups of Christians or churches, and probably to answer some need within those churches; in other words, they were writing within a religious and credal context, so what they wrote was strongly coloured by what they believed and what they felt needed to be said at the time. They allow us to see very little of Jesus the man – what he looked like, how he got on with his friends (anyway, it's doubtful if their sources would have recorded such things) – but instead they give us the supernatural Christ, the incarnate Word of God descending from heaven. They were also writing in the expectation of his imminent return, when God would wind up history and judgement would begin. So almost anything they report, and the way in which they report it, may be historical *or* may be a figurative way of expounding their theology or adapting known stories of Jesus so that they apply to contemporary problems. For example, when John reports that blood and water flowed from the side of Christ, is he simply reporting history, or is he writing to confute the people who claimed that Christ wasn't human, or is he talking about baptism (water) and the Eucharist (blood)? Or could he be referring to Zechariah's idea of the fountain of grace, or the Rabbinic tradition that connects Moses striking the rock to produce water with his act of turning water into blood; or is John referring to Jesus as the true Passover lamb?

One could go on and on. It is difficult to find anything like a parallel, but suppose that, in two thousand years' time, an archaeologist were to dig up a tiny scrap of a 1983 issue of *The Times* and read something like, 'Yesterday in the Commons the clock struck twelve for Mrs Thatcher and she was left in rags. How surprising, then, that it was Mr Kinnock who brought her her glass slipper . . .' You can imagine the learned articles that would emerge: 'The Uncomfortable and Slippery Footwear of Primitive Man', 'Timing Devices and Humiliation Ceremonies Amongst the Common Ancients', 'Foot Fetishism and the Growth of the Clock Industry', and so on. But until some other learned scholar unearthed a Cinderella papyrus, they wouldn't have a clue what had really been going on – and even then, would they really know? After all, perhaps they'd had a costume party that night and there really *was* a glass slipper . . .

There isn't room here to go into modern New Testament scholarship, except to say that many scholars of today would hesitate to claim certainty about the accuracy of the gospel records with regard to the historical Jesus; there are central strands which you can unravel and trace back with some degree of confidence, but what is presented in church as straight history/biography is in fact a highly complex mixture of theology, speculation, symbolism, reminiscence, encouragement, warning and so on. Furthermore, although we tend to think of the gospels as a monolith, as if they all said the same thing, in fact each presents a quite distinctive Christ. Any attempt to blend the different elements into a single portrait usually ends up denying important insights of the individual witnesses and presenting a Jesus remarkably similar to the 'ideal person' of the particular 'blender'. As William Blake pointed out, there is a danger of making Jesus in one's own image:

> The vision of Christ which Thou dost see
> Is my vision's greatest enemy.
> Thine has a great hook nose like Thine;
> Mine has a snub nose like mine.
> Thine is the friend of all mankind;
> Mine speaks in parables to the blind.

So we get hippy Jesuses, Victorian Jesuses, Sixties liberal Jesuses, gay Jesuses, repressive racist Jesuses, gentle-Jesus-meek-and-mild Jesuses, all the way to Hollywood Jesuses with capped teeth and peroxided hair, when really what we need to say is, 'This is Paul's Jesus, this Mark's, Matthew's, Luke's, John's, and each one is a different vision of God acting.'

It may come as a surprise, when you start to look at the New Testament records, to realise that the masses of credal material that we are expecting, all the things we feel we must believe, are nowhere to be found. We are looking into a world that hasn't yet had to work out precise definitions and formulae to explain the Jesus story. In particular, there is almost no mention of Jesus as God – that came later; what they did say, in many different ways, was that to have seen Jesus was to have seen God at work. The first person to write was St Paul, in his letters to various churches, doing his theology on the trot in response to particular situations, perhaps starting to write around AD 50, some twenty years after the death of Jesus. Paul shows no interest at all in Jesus as a person, nor in his history; what is central is the drama of Jesus' death and resurrection as the focus of God's decisive act in dealing with the forces which had separated man from God: 'Christ died for our sins, in accordance with the scriptures . . . he was buried . . . he was raised to life on the third day.' Paul sees the power of God at work in Jesus, restoring man's relationship with God.

Twenty years or so later comes the first of the gospels, that of St Mark, an ambiguous and mysterious little book whose author beavers away at trying to comprehend the link between suffering and salvation. Although deeply compassionate, Jesus is also an angry figure, misunderstood by his disciples who persist in underestimating the centrality of suffering; even his family and friends try to strait-jacket him because they think he is mad. Jesus dies with a cry of desperate loss – 'My God, my God, why hast thou forsaken me?' – and the gospel ends as abruptly as it began, with three women confronted by the empty tomb: 'They went out and ran away from the tomb, beside themselves with terror. They said nothing to anybody for they were afraid.' It was later generations, unable to cope with Mark's ambiguous and allusive approach, who felt they had to add the happy ending.

Some fifteen or twenty years later the author of Matthew wrote his gospel, using most of the material from the gospel of St Mark, but cutting out or changing awkward or embarrassing parts. He is not remotely interested in the mysterious side, but is more like a public school prefect, anxious to get the rules quite straight and to stick to them. Jesus becomes a sort of super-rabbi and his story is clearly marked with prophecy and fulfilment, rather as eggs used to have a little lion stamped on them to show that they were all right. Matthew introduces new chunks of material which probably came from a traditional source also shared by Luke. Parts of the gospel may well be examples of 'midrash', which was the contemporary technique for the exposition of scripture: expounding, expanding, explaining, creatively meditating around the stark and (in Matthew's eyes) potentially dangerous and unorthodox work of Mark's gospel.

Luke's gospel is probably everyone's favourite, because his Jesus is the most warmly human. Unlike Matthew's churchy head-boy approach, Luke's is much more secular and commonsensical, fleshed out with beautiful stories like the Good Samaritan, the Prodigal Son, the annunciation, and the shepherds at the manger. It is a humanistic story of the triumph of heroic virtue. When Jesus dies, instead of being mocked by the two thieves who were crucified with him, as Mark and Matthew report, he becomes the friend of the dying thief. And his final words are not of despair but of committal to God – 'Father, into thy hands I commit my spirit.' When people try to make a *mélange* of the different gospel portraits, it's not surprising that Luke's human and humane hero should usually be the main ingredient.

And lastly John, the very opposite of Luke. Luke chose to tell a story, and to a certain extent his theological concepts are subordinated to his narrative needs. For John, the narrative is the servant of the theology, which may explain why his story is often at complete odds with the other three gospels. His language is allusive and illusive, often working on many different levels, and his picture of Jesus is perhaps the most difficult for us to understand, edging as it does towards Docetism – the idea that Christ only seemed to be human, but was actually divine. Thus Jesus' death is really his glorification, his last words are ones of calm triumph – 'It is finished' – and the words 'gave up his spirit' at the point of death imply a conscious act on his part; it was something he chose to do. You cannot be sure where John stands, whether he sees the world as good or bad, whether the important theme of the prologue is the idea of 'flesh', the earthliness of Jesus, or the light bursting in on the world, something alien from outside. At the raising of Lazarus the two levels of human and divine clash awkwardly together: 'Lazarus is dead. I am glad not to have been there; it will be for your good and for the good of your faith.' (Can you imagine Luke's Jesus saying anything so cold or calculating?) And yet when Jesus reaches the mourners, 'he sighed heavily and was deeply moved . . . Jesus wept.' In the other gospels, Jesus proclaims the Kingdom of God and only lays his own claims indirectly. In John, Jesus proclaims himself, and the miracles are not performed in response to faith, as a sign of God's kingdom breaking into the world, but in order to awaken faith in Jesus or to manifest his glory.

But if all four gospels are different, which one is telling the truth, which one can we be most certain about? Perhaps the answer is that, rather than trying to toss up between them, or trying to blend them into a convincing whole, we should accept their individuality; we should let them get on with the job and with what they want to tell us. And if that means perplexity and uncertainty, so be it; we said that revelation must be ambiguous if it isn't to be a bludgeon, but perhaps we would secretly prefer to be bludgeoned – at least then we could be sure. But what happened, then, to all our good intentions to follow Lessing in the active quest for truth (because 'absolute truth is for you alone')?

We have to accept that we are not faced with simple histories as we understand them ('Then Montgomery approached El Alamein and Rommel deployed × tanks . . .'), but with people who were working within the framework of Hebrew thought, where history and theology were inextricably intertwined: it is event *plus* interpretation, and as that interpretation involves understanding the mighty acts of God in history, the languages of fact, speculation and worship are all interrelated. To us it may sometimes feel like cheating, but to the people of that time and place it was the accepted way of doing things. If you see a TV road-safety advertisement showing a child running across the road, it's untrue in the sense that the incident never really happened, but it is a sort of 'midrash' or expounding of the plain words of the safety code in a way that will make them more immediate, memorable and understandable. To have left God, the theologically interpretative and worshipful element, out of the picture, would have been as bizarre and naive to the gospel-writers or Jewish historians as a road-safety film would be to us without any cars. We have to learn to live with the uncertainty in the gospels between where the facts end and the interpretation begins; and who knows but that the interpretation may involve facts which the 1980s have forgotten to take into account?

For us, 'the truth,' as dear Oscar said, 'is rarely pure, and never simple'. It's hard enough to know what is *actually* happening this week, let alone two thousand years ago; but even if one still clings to the hope of the gospels as simple historical records, what then? The problem is that it is difficult to see how a historical figure can have any relevance to the here and now. I know that Julius Caesar invaded

Britain, but it doesn't make much difference to the problems and realities of my life. In the same way, what difference would it make to my life if I could put my hand on my heart and swear that I am certain that every word written about Jesus in the gospels is objective fact? Take miracles – raising the dead, walking on the water, resurrection – if we demand to see these purely as fact, what is the result? The danger is that it can be very similar to what happens if we demand to know the existence of God as fact: we are back on the treadmill of security/certainty. If I can be a hundred per cent sure that Jesus rose from the dead, then I need not feel so afraid of dying; if I can be a hundred per cent sure that the miracles happened, then I shall know that everything will be all right in the end. So I can relax about problems of personal survival and meaning, and concentrate on forming a good relationship with the power source.

There are probably thousands of non-Christians who assume that the story of Jesus is more or less true – give or take the odd miracle – and they are probably prepared to agree that something extraordinary happened after his death, but this knowledge has as much effect on their lives as knowing about the existence of the Great Wall of China. If it were proved conclusively that the Turin shroud was the shroud of Jesus and that its chemical composition can only be explained by his resurrection, some people might start drifting into church, but what would be bringing them? If the Church is based merely on historical certainty, what more has it to offer than the possibility of backing a winner? It wouldn't relate any more closely to the central realities of people's lives as they experience them; it would just be another pressure from outside, another form of God 'out there'.

The problem is that the question of Jesus has always tended to be explained in terms of the historical – Did he exist or not? Is this story true or not? – when what we should have been saying is that it is not a question of the merely historical, but rather that the historical has furnished the basis for a myth or blueprint which points to the nature of existence and what it means to be human. As Maynard Mack wrote of tragedy, it 'never tells us what to think; it shows us what we are and may be'. Perhaps there was an intake of breath at the word 'myth' – does it mean that it isn't true? But I'm using the word in the sense that Jung does, namely that a myth is a story encapsulating a truth too complex to be explained in any other way. Something quite specific happened in history, but its meaning and importance are more than merely specific; its significance is universal and can only be validated, not by the process of historical analysis – as if it were still and only something in the past – but by taking it as a blueprint or lens with which to apprehend one's existence and by which to choose to live one's life. Otherwise we fall back into the trap of making the religious life a question of believing – I believe in God, whatever that means; I believe that Jesus walked on the water, whatever that means, and whatever relevance that may have to my life – rather than making the religious life a question of being, how one lives one's life, how one tries to follow the blueprint of sacrificial love. It is almost the attitude of Henri Matisse: 'I don't know whether I believe in God or not. I think, really, I'm some sort of Buddhist. But the essential thing is to put oneself in a frame of mind which is close to that of prayer.' He defies, or is disinterested in, categorisation – 'I don't know . . . I think . . . some sort of . . ., – but 'the *essential* thing' is how one chooses to live.

So how does one choose to live by the Christian blueprint? If we reject the idea of a God out there, coming to earth as a human being, what are we left with? Not much, according to some people. Certainly there is an image of Jesus that dies hard, where the human side is almost squashed out of sight by the divine, and you are left with a figure like one of those monsters in science fiction movies, externally identical to a human being, but an alien inside; it's hard to see what such a creature could have to say to us today. Yet our problem is nothing new; the Church has always been wrestling with the enigma of Jesus; you only have to look at the plethora of titles and images in the New Testament to see how the writers were striving to explore the mystery of Christ – Messiah, Son of Man, Son of God, The Christ, Word, Lord, Lamb of God, and so on. And then the Church carried on the exploration – a divine being who 'usefully pretended to suffer', an ordinary man adopted by God; Nestorianism, Appolinarianism, Arianism, and so forth. The final formula wasn't agreed upon until the Council of Nicaea in AD 325, about three hundred years after Christ's death, and even then it was an uneasy and ambiguous compromise which had to be reached with an agitated Emperor Constantine breathing down the delegates' necks.

And we have as many different models to deal with today – if we're interested enough. There's Jesus as the charismatic historical figure or the great human teacher, or as another example of life's tragedy, or as the worthy figurehead of what has become a retrograde superstition, or as the sacred mushroom who ends up as King of France (I never did understand that book), or as the central figure of a cult of personal devotion – the list is endless. Perhaps, rather than being the key dot in the puzzle picture, Jesus turns out to be a complete puzzle picture himself. Here again, I think I can see a pattern which forms the basis for my blueprint, but my pattern may be random and meaningless for anyone else. If we allow ourselves to be confronted by the mystery of Christ, we each have to spend our lives trying to trace our own pattern. But the more we allow ourselves to be distracted by the God-ward side of Christ, the more we may be tempted to ignore the search into the meaning of his humanity – a humanity that holds in coded form the meaning of what it is to be truly human.

What *do* we know about Jesus? What is the basis of our blueprint? Well, everyone knows what we are *supposed* to think: he was true God and true man. I'd prefer to leave the theologians to grapple over what exactly that might mean, and perhaps substitute a slightly different model (though I want to come back later to two very important truths which the God/man picture implies). Rather than thinking of God as another being, approaching him like interested or bored spectators peering through a microscope for clues, I suggested earlier that the question of God has more to do with the nature of existence and our experience of meaning: in this we are not passive spectators but participants – our lives either have or have not meaning. Nor are our lives static;

man is not a fixed quantity but a dynamic entity, on the move. Rather than being alien to ourselves, introduced from outside, or like us but with the extra plus-ingredient injected into him from outside (the 'new blue whitener'), Jesus is actually the signpost to where man should be going; he is the meeting-place between humanity – what it is to be truly human in all its potential – and Being itself; the meaning of human existence is revealed in him, for those who have eyes to see.

This approach preserves a central Christian truth, also contained in the God/man model, which religion sometimes chooses to forget, namely, the absolute worth and beauty of the human personality; if you say that God became man, you are making the most enormous value claims for the stature and worth of manhood. Unfortunately, the God/man model can also work in the opposite direction by forcing an unhealthy split between God, the infinite creator, and man, the finite creature; according to this reading, which can be sweetly seductive to the neurotic guilt factor in us all, man is really a mass of sin, lust and evil and disgusting desires (have you ever noticed how some preachers' eyes light up when they start cataloguing sins, especially of the flesh? It's obviously a complete turn-on. And I'm not even going to mention the religious orders which go in for flagellation . . .).

The patron saints of this approach are Adam and Eve, and the idea is that we should all rush around feeling intensely guilty for being human because of the Fallen Nature of Man, Original Sin and other goodies. Even though most people have long ago given up any thought of the Garden of Eden as something that really existed, the memory lingers on in Christian doctrine, so that you get a scenario of man being created finitely perfect, then choosing to destroy it all and plunge himself into sin and misery, from which we still suffer; and we share Adam's guilt just by being human. 'You only have to look at the way a young baby behaves,' said the preacher one Sunday, 'to see that man's nature is basically selfish and impure'. As Milton put it:

> Of man's first disobedience, and the fruit
> Of that forbidden tree, whose mortal taste

> Brought death into the world, and all our woe
> With loss of Eden . . .

Jesus is then introduced into mankind from outside –
although not really human himself because he doesn't share
in original sin and is completely faultless – and according to a
variety of different models, he goes some way towards
healing the breach between God and man. The squeamish
and the non-Christians will perhaps forgive me if I list as
follows some of the versions of what happened on the cross:
the devil had to have his due but was cheated of his prey by
Christ taking the punishment meant for mankind; or justice
demanded that mankind should be punished and so God had
to punish someone; or God's wrath had to be appeased and
Jesus bore the brunt of it; or Jesus' death was the only way
to pay off the vast backlog of accumulated sin and evil, as if
God were so puny that he needed to stage an historical
incident to get his work of reconciliation started, or such a
tyrant that he needed a sacrifice to turn him from being
angry to gracious – that's the behaviour of a spoiled child.
There are some scraps of truth lurking around under all that
nastiness that we may need to pick out later, but if we don't
believe in Adam and Eve, or in Jesus coming from 'out
there', hopefully we can turn our backs on such barbarities.

There is another approach in Christian thinking, still
based on Adam and Eve but far closer to our own thinking
in this post-Darwinian world. Irenaeus, Bishop of Lyons,
who lived during the latter part of the second century AD,
suggested that, far from being created perfect and thence
falling away from perfection, man was actually created as
imperfect and immature, and it was only after a period of
growth, maturation and learning to distinguish good from
evil, that man would gradually grow into the likeness of
God. Surely this idea of upward growth, of man being called
into fulness of being, is far closer to everything we have been
saying about the dynamic nature of man. And if we stick to
this approach, then Jesus becomes, not a rescuer from
outside to remind us of how awful we are, but an explorer, a
challenge to mankind as to what we should become, a
pointer to our most basic nature. So Irenaeus says that the

Holy Spirit 'purifies man and raises him up to the Life of God', and Theophilus of Antioch wrote, 'Man was created with the possibility of progress so that he might advance and ascend into heaven.' The author of the Second Letter of Peter in the New Testament talks of coming 'to share in the very being of God', and perhaps most dramatically, St Athanasius writes of Jesus, 'He was made man that we might be made God.'

Perhaps the reason why we cling to talk of the fallen nature of man, even though we know the fall is only a story, is that it helps to contain our real experience of the cumulative power of evil and negativity in our lives and also our sense of the total qualitative difference between ourselves and holy Being when it reveals itself to us. In a world that produces Hitler and Stalin and where Sartre can write, without fear of mockery, 'Hell is other people', only an idiot would deny the constant pressure of non-being. But surely we don't need an old myth to explain that, particularly when it is a myth that seems to tarnish the very idea of being human. If one uses the model of growth, of man being called into fulness of being, then we know that there is the constant risk that he may ignore that call and fall back into non-being; we know too that there must be a tragic element in creation itself because it is always at risk, always capable of being rejected.

The warden of a hostel for battered wives and children told me that she cried more for the husbands than for their families, because although the families were victims, they had the chance of escape and new growth, whereas the husbands were victims of a violence and negativity within themselves which they couldn't escape and which came to dominate them. Sin, the power of negativity in our lives, isn't a process that we can stop or start at will, but something that can take on a momentum and life of its own:

> Action is transitory, – a step, a blow,
> The motion of a muscle, this way or that –
> 'Tis done, and in the after vacancy
> We wonder at ourselves like men betrayed:

> Suffering is permanent, obscure and dark,
> And shares the nature of infinity.
>
> (Wordsworth: The Borderers)

Sometimes Sin isn't even a state started by us – it is an ongoing process that we are caught up in. Men who batter their families were often battered themselves as children: violence is a pattern of behaviour that they were processed into at an early age – they don't just switch it on and off at will. None of this is to do with some prehistoric fairy story; it is a fact of life that man lives in the tension between being and non-being, meaning and meaninglessness. Getting caught up in some primordial guilt complex does nothing to help us get on with the job of being human.

I wrote earlier about two important truths which the God/ man picture contains. The first was about the *value* of being human, the second encapsulates the *problem* of being human. To link God and man is to say that nothing solely man-made will ever be enough for us. Writers from the Third World warn us about seeing technology as the only answer to their problems, because it may only produce yet more nations of consumers, rather than creators of history and human values. Technology, they say, creates a false man who sees life in terms of what the system will give him, and happiness in terms of what he can possess. In the same way, Laurens Van Der Post reports talking to holy men from all over the world – a Zulu prophet, a Zen priest and so on – who say that their people have lost any sense of belonging or meaning: they talk only in terms of what is 'useful' to them, and what they can possess.

So the God side of the God/man equation stands for the need to assert man's quest for more than the merely material; even if the whole world were warmly clothed and fed and watered and surrounded by creature comforts, would we be any nearer knowing what it means to be a man, or any nearer to satisfying the depths and transcendence of his nature?

But the man side of the God/man equation is an important counter balance, warning us that we must not float off into heavenly speculation, pietism, pie in the sky. Jesus was a man, and so the whole human race should be of central and vital importance to us; far from being consumed with guilt about being human, we should rejoice in it and be prepared to fight hard against all that goes to make people less than human: disease, hunger, war, political oppression, fanaticism – and religion that makes the world out to be something bad and dirty, rather than the creation of God, of Being. The God/man model tells us that we must never dare to make humanity anything less than our ultimate concern because it was in a man that the face of God was revealed, but we must also fight against all that denies the transcendent in man, because without it he only has half a meaning.

If Jesus had died at a ripe old age in the prophet's retirement home, would anyone remember him now? Or would he be lost in the back annals of Jewish history along with other miracle workers like Honi the circle-drawer, or perhaps honoured as a minor prophet? But he died terribly, defeated, betrayed and abandoned by his followers. The frightening thing about the Christian message is that it has nothing to do with our wandering around looking pious and wonderful (the Action Man Pale Galilean Kit), but focuses our attention on the cross, on suffering. Here, it says, is the key to meaning.

When the first gospel writer, Mark, came to write his theology of Jesus, he made space for miracles, of course, but he also veiled them with secrecy almost as if they could not be understood without reference to something far more important – the theme that he weaves throughout his gospel, worrying away at it to give up its secret – the theme of suffering. So Mark devotes a third of his whole book to the story of Jesus' final suffering and death and the build-up to it, underlining its vital importance; from the very beginning he plants clues and allusions to the Passion, so that the whole course of Jesus' ministry is seen to relate to that moment.

When Matthew and Luke came to write their gospels, whereas they felt free to alter Mark's stories of Jesus' ministry as much as they wanted to, when it came to the Passion story they stepped back, as if it were too central and too important for them to tinker with. And the Passion story is the mystery at the heart of the Christian religion. Once again we find ourselves confronted by the cross, and once again there are no cosy answers to hand – it is merely a terrible instance of human folly, or it is something more, but nothing I can do or say would convince anyone either way, nor can you just try it on for size: the cross confronts you, and in the end you either have to shrug your shoulders and wander off muttering, 'Stupid waste of time', or you have to start on the long road of struggle and dialectic with the cross. 'The folly of the Gospel,' Paul called it, 'Jews call for miracles, Greeks look for wisdom; but we proclaim Christ – yes, Christ nailed to the cross; and though this is a stumbling-block to Jews and folly to Greeks, yet to those who have heard his call, Jews and Greeks alike, he is the power of God and the wisdom of God.'

In other words, although it may simply be a blueprint of the absurdity and pain of existence, the cross is the blueprint of what being is about. If God is good for anything, then this is where the answer will be found; and if our lives are not to crumble under the pressure of absurdity, then the answer must be here, too. So we start digging again, at what G.K. Chesterton called 'that terrible tree, which is the death of God and the life of man'.

4. The death of God and the life of man

Can I try to piece together some of what we have been saying so far, to give us some sort of perspective with which to approach the cross? Perhaps diffidence is the most important angle – diffidence about being certain.

In the first chapter we looked at some of the many ways in which we try to protect our lives from anxiety; one of those ways is God, and, in order for him to act as the best of all possible comfort blankets, we demand to be quite certain about him, and especially whether or not he exists: religion becomes a question of knowing and promoting 'facts' rather than a way of living and of apprehending one's existence. I suggested in various ways that arguing whether or not God 'exists' is to ask the wrong sort of question – in a sense, who cares anyway? The important question is whether or not our lives have a meaning and context beyond the immediate; and to that there can be no certain answer. We may simply be another species programmed to reproduce as effectively as possible, or we may be more: all along, we've said that life is ambiguous.

To be aware of that ambiguity, not to expect clear-cut answers from life, seems to me a sure sign of mankind growing out of its leading-strings. If there *is* meaning, or if we can sense it in our lives, then that should be enough for us: to start looking for more brings possible problems of self-seeking, reward and personal survival, when it should be enough simply to want to live the most loving life possible, because in the end that is the only meaningful life. Talk of God can be dangerously distracting from the here and now. So we approach the cross with diffidence, not asking for certainty or proof, but perhaps looking for the key to what it means to to live *the most loving life possible*.

This diffidence extends also to our view of Jesus. The

historical man is obscured from us and it's a risky business to start running to him for certainty, because we may end up ignoring the *mysterium*, the God-ward side, and worshipping someone we have imagined in our own image. And what of the theology of who or what Jesus was? What we have really been saying is that the word 'God' is a symbol, and to link Jesus with God is not to create a strange mythical creature half one thing, half another, like a centaur, but an attempt to understand an experience that by its very nature can't be codified. Perhaps we can learn from the Old Testament and Judaism here, when they say *you must not conceptualize God* – God is not a concept, but the living *experience* of the Jewish people. When the Roman general Pompeius entered the Jewish temple he was stunned to find that it was empty – but how do you carve a statue of the experience of being challenged and given grace, the free gift of God's perfect love?

Similarly with Jesus, the more you try to tie him down in words, the further you get from the experience of being confronted by him. We cannot know for certain how he thought of himself (and as we saw from the four different portraits in the gospels, the old saying, 'He was either mad, bad or God', is too simplistic really to work), but what we can say is that in his life and death some people became radically aware of the challenge and promise implicit in existence. So, with diffidence, we tried to move away from the notion of Jesus coming from 'out there' or of his being in some way different from humanity, just as we had tried to get rid of the idea of a God 'out there' and moved towards the idea of all creation being instinct with the holy – pan-en-theism, God's presence in all creation – and consequently we arrived at the idea of religion or Jesus or God not being set apart from us but being the whole spectrum of our existence as lived in them.

I suppose what I'm trying to say is that we should be able to relax about God and about Jesus. Instead of getting neurotic and worried about them, as if they somehow need protecting (like infantile fears about one's parents dying?), why can't we relax and have trust in Being? If God is Being-itself, the ground of all reality, then we should expect and hope to meet him anywhere and everywhere, and perhaps in the most unexpected and unwanted places. For the Christian, the meeting-place is Christ, but I have no intention of trying to give him a good reference so that the reader can assess him, like trying on a hat. I don't think we can question Christ; he questions us in the same way that Peter was questioned in the apocryphal story where he was fleeing from persecution and met the risen Lord: '*Quo vadis?*' – 'Where are you going?' Jesus confronts us with the same question.

As anxiety, as Kierkegaard saw it, enters and searches the soul, leading us where we need to go, so Jesus is the lodestone and the lodestar, the guiding principle, the object of pursuit, the one who draws us on our journey. William Law wrote about the whole of our life being something that exercises the 'Spirit and life of Christ in the soul . . . From morning to night keep Jesus in thy heart, long for nothing, desire nothing, but to have all that is within thee changed into the Spirit and temper of the holy Jesus.' In other words, stop wondering what we can get out of it, perhaps even whether it's true or not, and get on with your journey in the light of Christ.

But if we believe in 'the sanctification of all things', Jesus is not an old hat that you may or may not try on for size – he is there already, even if unseen, unknown, unrecognised. That is why some of my agnostic, Jewish or atheist friends seem to me to lead profoundly Christian lives. They are not baptised, they don't believe in Jesus, and they would feel (very rightly) that I was patronising them if I said that they lived like Christians; but I believe that active in them is the same 'power not ourselves making for righteousness' that was at work in Jesus. Perhaps Christians need to learn to trust God and rejoice that the creative power of Being is at work everywhere, instead of jealously trying to keep it to ourselves, hemmed in by rules and regulations, and then wondering why we feel so miserable and alone.

So we approach the cross with diffidence – not asking for certainty, and not claiming to have all the answers. But with hope too, because 'the death of God and the life of man', as Chesterton called it, means that perhaps the cross can be the starting-point for mankind come-of-age, trying not to hide behind the omnipotent God-out-there, and trying to take in the beautiful fact that holy, creative Being is here instinct in every one of us – teaching us what it means to *live*. 'I have come that men may have life, and may have it in all its fullness.'

In 1983 the Royal Academy in London exhibited the Cimabue crucifix, a vast wooden structure, painted in the thirteenth century and severely damaged in the Florence flood of 1966. Large areas of the paintwork were destroyed by the floodwaters, so that the image of Christ is partly obscured – there are big blank patches on his face and body but the dramatic impact of the curve of his body is undiminished. The fine detail is lost to us, but the pathos remains. It is like a huge brooding monument exciting the classic response to tragedy – pity and terror – pity, making us draw near; terror, making us recoil: the same reactions inspired in us by the *mysterium tremendum et fascinans*.

If you walk to the back of the crucifix, the glamour of the interpretative artistry is all gone; instead we have a solid structure of ancient wooden beams and crossbeams, still enormous and overpowering, but also rough and workmanlike – it has its job to do, and it gets on with it without any reference to anyone else. When we start to contemplate the cross of Christ, we too want to get to the original truth behind the artistry of the gospels, but that door is closed to us; the solid workmanlike reality of those actual wooden beams and the people round them is inaccessible. So we have to rely on the artists and their vision – the creative and dramatic picture presented to us.

And yet even what they had to say has been obscured and defaced by the floodwaters of time; what is left to us is the dramatic sweep of the story, and the effect it has on us. It's pointless now to stand in front of a partly obscured masterpiece and start analysing it; what is important is how it affects the way we perceive the world and the way we act in that world. The experts, perhaps, will constantly need to reassess what the picture is doing in technical terms, but as we said before when talking about art, analysis of the technical side may help us to understand something of the 'how' of a work of art, but very little of the 'why' – the question it poses us, what it communicates to us.

Before the Cimabue crucifix was damaged, the watcher's gaze was drawn upwards by the curve of Christ's body to his eyes, and from there to the figure of God watching over him. The flood damaged that natural upward movement, broke it and obscured it – now our gaze remains fixed on the half obliterated face of the suffering man, his eyes closed in secret and terrible pain. God is no longer part of the picture. On the arms of the cross, the faces of Mary and St John look out at the spectator, begging our sympathy and involvement in this tragic spectacle. If God is there now, he is in the broken man, not hovering overhead uninvolved.

The room where the crucifix was displayed was totally unlike that of any other exhibition I have seen. It was more like a holy place, full of people standing or sitting in silence, gazing at the cross. But it wasn't just the art of human pity that held them; unhindered by the trappings of God or religion or pious thoughts, the cross spoke to them and seemed to touch some core deep within them. After long minutes of silent contemplation, they would move slowly away. But what did it say to them? I can't answer for them, and I doubt if they would have wanted to put such an experience into words anyway, but it was as if something there made sense to them, as if it were a place where the pieces began to fit together.

And for the Christian, the cross is the place where he looks for understanding of life and of himself. It is the most complete statement we have, or the most vivid clue, as to the nature of being. It is also the challenge that tells us where we need to go in order to be in touch with the deepest levels of our own reality.

What do we see of Being in such a place? For a start, we need to dispose of the uninvolved spectator God; the cross is the death of God as judge eternal throned in splendour. What you become aware of is that Being, pouring forth into all beings, is at risk. At its most dramatic, if we blew up the world in a nuclear holocaust, wouldn't all of Being that has put itself at risk in manifesting itself in created things, then be confronted by non-being, amputation, loss of part of itself? The cross is partly a statement of that risk, but it is also a clue to the fundamental nature of Being and so to our own deepest reality, because we are all part of Being.

Bearing in mind that words are only symbols to help us guess at the unguessable, the image of Being that you get from the cross is love: suffering, sacrificial, risk-taking, involved, committed, creative love. It's the same image that you get from the life of Jesus: someone who didn't separate religion and life into neat little compartments, but lived his life to the full, passionately committed to the life and growth of everyone he met. He spent himself constantly in going out to people and meeting them in their need, accepting and loving them completely, even when they murdered him. Love, the 'active concern for the life and growth of that which we love' (Erich Fromm), is a risky business because it involves making yourself vulnerable to others, open to be hurt by them, and it involves spending yourself. If you take the cross as your marker, you are saying that you glimpse something of that love in the fundamental nature of existence.

This experience of love and acceptance was felt so strongly by the first Christians that they had to find a new word for it. Up until then there were two interchangeable words for love, *eros* and *agape*. The Christians took over *agape*, and gave it a new meaning. *Eros* means, essentially, love with conditions attached, demanding love, grasping love – the sort of thing we give and receive all our lives. I love you because you are beautiful, sexy, a fantastic cook and look good beside me at parties; you love me because of my fraying Irish charm. We all experience conditional love as children: 'I love you because you live up to my expectations, pass your exams, don't wet the bed . . .' Society loves us if we live up to what it wants from us. All these (often unspoken) demands of parents, society, friends can become projected onto Father God, so that we feel we have to behave or be in a certain way in order to reach or be acceptable to the deity. *Agape* is the complete reversal of this, without any 'ifs' or 'buts' or conditions. There is no watchful parent or judge to appease – there is the perhaps more difficult task of learning to accept that Being is at work in us, and that when we give ourselves in love we are simply echoing the activity of that Being within us.

Easier said than done, however, and the message of the cross is not conducive to a quiet mind. The challenging paradoxes of the cross sound so unbelievable, but the closer you look at the cross, the more they sound at you: you have to die to yourself in order to live; you have to give before you can really receive; what you keep you lose; if you dare to lose yourself you will find yourself; the more secure you make yourself, the more insecure you will be; unless you let go and trust you will be your own prisoner; until you let go of God and confront absurdity and the pressure of the shadow in yourself and the world, you will never meet God.

Kierkegaard talks of 'the Two Ways: one is to suffer; the other is to become a professor of the fact that another suffered'. Perhaps the second way concerns the God 'out there', the useless, cruel God that the widow in the prologue felt I was bringing her for cheap consolation, the God that some religion teaches us we should become professors of, academics clinging on to 'facts' about something far, far away that we can't understand and which may in the end rob us of our humanity. The first way, on the other hand, has to do with the way of paradox, the road we are called to follow if we take the cross seriously, trying to incarnate sacrificial love in the world.

But how? How can we possibly do it? The life of Jesus gives a clue, but there are dangers here because, in our anxiety about the challenge of freedom, it is often tempting to try to be anyone rather than ourselves. The imitation of Christ – trying to follow the blueprint that Christ sets before each of us individually – can become identification with Christ, abandoning our own journey to try and be someone else, in this case our image of what we would like Jesus to have been, and glorifying 'self-sacrifice' when what we are really doing is avoiding at all costs the greater sacrifice of being real. The blueprint of Jesus is about reality, about someone very human who lived absolutely consistently by his own truth and reality. In the truest sense, he was the hero of his own life.

But here we need to introduce a warning, perhaps symbol-ised by the story of Jesus' temptation by the devil. In a sense, the temptation was to make himself and his own glory the end product; Jesus rejected this because he was in search of a truth and a reality beyond his own. He could only serve this truth by being true to himself, true to his vision. For us, the devil's name is egoism, and we shall need to come back to him when we try to disentangle those great Christian paradoxes and to see why self-love has nothing to do with narcissism; but for the moment we must try to look more closely at the questions posed by the story of Jesus.

Here was a man who lived his life in response to the call of love. To be true to this call, to the journey set before him, he risked alienating friends and family and overturning the accepted religious beliefs of the time. He was open to everyone he met, without side or prejudice. If he felt that someone needed a good kick in the pants to shock him out of his self-righteousness, he was only too happy to oblige; if a prostitute needed to know that she was loved and accepted for herself as a person, not as a piece of flesh, then he gave her that acceptance regardless of the raised eyebrows and the scandalised religious. He gave his followers a startlingly new vision of authority, based on humility and service, and in the service of his mission to mankind he was faithful until death – a death whose keynote was complete forgiveness, love returned for hatred. After his death he left a scattered band of disillusioned and hopeless followers most of whom, if we follow Mark, had never really grasped what he was on about anyway. But then something happened that changed this band of frightened failures into a group with drive, purpose and confidence, and making the most extraordinary claims. Something happened which caused them to set off round the world to spread the good news, to face persecu-tion and martyrdom, to say that God had acted in Jesus: 'God has made him both Lord and Christ, this Jesus whom you crucified.' Their experience of death, defeat and failure in Christ and themselves was changed into one of triumph. God, they said, had raised Jesus from the dead.

But what can we make of a phenomenon so totally outside

our own experience of life and so contrary to all the laws of
nature? Was the talk of resurrection simply their way of
saying that they felt everything that Jesus stood for had been
validated? I've seen graffiti in Cyprus saying 'Makarios
lives', which really mean 'Makarios was right, and I stand by
everything he worked for.' But is it enough just to say that?
Would the whole explosion of the early Church have stem-
med from such a colossal defeat if there hadn't been
something else as well? It is impossible for us to tell, but
what we can do, and what is more important, is to try to
understand it or experience it in the context of our own lives
– otherwise we're right back to being professors again. We
have to accept that it's impossible for us to get back to the
historical truth of what actually happened; what we have to
do is to find out if resurrection will work as a symbol for
something true of our own experience of life. So here again,
we don't believe or disbelieve in the resurrection – that's not
what's important – but we test out the idea in our lives. We
need to remember Hemingway's warning, though: 'There
are some things which cannot be learned quickly, and time –
which is all we have – must be paid heavily for their
acquiring.'

Whatever happened to Jesus after his death has got to
make sense in the context of his life and ministry, otherwise
it's just a freak event, of as much spiritual value as Yuri
Geller bending forks. The life, death and resurrection of
Jesus are the key points in the blueprint of which we have
spoken: a life lived in obedience to a call, asking people to
take themselves seriously – to pay attention to themselves. It
is vitally important to understand the way Jesus went about
his ministry, if we are indeed to follow him.

We might take as a key the opening words of Dickens'
David Copperfield: 'Whether I shall turn out to be the hero
of my own life, or whether that station will be held by
anybody else, these pages must show.' Now the idea of
seeing oneself as the hero of one's life starts ringing all those
alarm bells about narcissism, self-love and so on, but the
whole point about the true hero is not that he sits around all
day polishing his armour and admiring his reflection in his
shield, but that he is someone in search of his truth, who has

to undergo danger, suffering and solitude on his quest, and who in the end finds new being. While others stay at home in search of happiness, following the line of least resistance and perhaps surrendering to fantasies and to the need to win the approval of society, the hero follows the task set him by life and in doing so – as a by-product, *not* as an end-product – grows into the fullness of his being, becomes whole. Jung describes the experience of wholeness thus: 'They came to themselves, they could accept themselves, they were able to become reconciled to themselves, and thus were reconciled to adverse circumstances and events. This is almost like what used to be expressed by saying: He has made his peace with God, he has sacrificed his own will, he has submitted to the will of God.'

So Jesus cured sickness and cared for souls, not by magic but by the integrity of his own personality, by living his own life to the utmost, preaching, hiking, telling stories, chatting, fighting, touching, praying, visiting, dining, sharing, crying, comforting, agonising, suffering, dying: All around him people were stirred into action, forced to live up to the best or worst in themselves, surrendering to the old life of compromise or finding new life.

Jung wrote about 'the way of individuation' and the opposite path, the 'flight from the final consequences of one's own being', hiding behind moral, social, religious and political conventions. Those are exactly the conventions that Jesus' opponents hid behind, and in a sense who can blame them? Anything for a quiet life. What they were resisting so strongly was the chance of new life, but as Kierkegaard saw, that is deeply threatening. How disturbing to meet one of the people Jung describes who 'towered up like mountain peaks above the mass that still clung to its collective fears, its beliefs, laws, and systems, and boldly chose their own way. To the man in the street it has always seemed miraculous that anyone should turn aside from the beaten track with its known destinations, and strike out on the steep and narrow path leading into the unknown.'

Jesus' loyalty to his truth led him on to the cross and to this strange Christian paradox: that we believe that it was precisely when he was at his most broken, most defeated, most empty, most helpless, that he accomplished the most – the supreme example of God's words to Paul, 'My power comes to its full strength in weakness.' The Christian symbol of triumph is an instrument of defeat and torture. And what are we to make of this? It is the sign that Jesus, as hero, was prepared to empty himself of everything – all that we think goes to make up a self – for the sake of his quest. Stripped of power, success, possessions, friends, hope for the future, stripped of everything except love; wrists nailed to wood, as helpless as a baby, unable even to grasp anything or move in any way except in that ghastly see-saw motion of taking the weight of your body first on your nailed feet, then on your wrists as the pain becomes unbearable. This see-saw motion was detected on the skeleton of a crucified man, having worn away part of the wrist-bone where it met the nail. Emptied of hope, even perhaps of belief in God – because what else does it mean to cry out that God has abandoned you? – he was left to confront death in loyalty to his quest. This emptying, this brokenness, was also the supreme example of his freedom from self, his concern only for others. And the resurrection is the validation of this; it is the promise that letting the self be put to death in the cause of love, leads to the birth of the true self, glorious, whole, transfiguring, bringing new life for others.

Fine words, but do they really mean anything? The problem is that we can't even begin to understand what resurrection may be about until we've first let ourselves be crucified. But there is an example from our own time which may help us to understand a little more clearly. A Jewish psychotherapist called Viktor Frankl was confronted by our modern crucifixion – internment in a Nazi concentration camp. He too was rendered helpless, family wiped out, the manuscript of his life's work destroyed, confronted with one of the most evil, agonising and meaningless existences that man has been able to devise. My friend who has the tattoo marks from Buchenwald on her wrist, or those who have been to Yad Vashem in Jerusalem, the memorial of the holocaust, might be able to give us the smallest inkling of just how evil and meaningless it was.

Like the hero, Frankl took as his theme Nietzsche's

words, 'He who has a *why* to live can bear with almost any *how*.' Emptied of everything, all human hopes and possibilities, Frankl, like Jesus, was left with the last of the human freedoms, the ability to choose one's attitude in any given set of circumstances – in Frankl's case, to choose how to confront this existence of nightmare and despair. From the poverty of knowing we have 'nothing to lose except our so ridiculously naked lives', he came to make sense out of the senselessness of his suffering, and to understand that to live is to suffer. Our task is to find meaning in that suffering, but no one can give us the answer; we each have to find our own answer and to accept the responsibility that this lays on us. And this applies to all mankind, not just to those trying to survive in a concentration camp.

> We had to learn . . . that it did not really matter what we expected from life, but rather what life expected from us. We needed to stop asking about the meaning of life, and instead to think of ourselves as those who were being questioned by life – daily and hourly. Our answer must consist, not in talk and meditation, but in right conduct. Life ultimately means taking the responsibility to find the right answer to its problems and to fulfil the tasks which it constantly sets for each individual.

Frankl had his face ground into the cross of meaning and meaninglessness, but on his release from the camp after the war he experienced what I can only call resurrection; he came out of hell believing that *good is indestructible*, in the end more real than evil: 'Our generation is realistic for we have come to know man as he really is. After all, man is that being who has invented the gas chambers of Auschwitz; however, he is also that being who has entered those gas chambers upright, with the Lord's Prayer or the Shema Yisrael on his lips.'

Can we now try to unravel those great Christian paradoxes, the promise that Jesus on the cross gives to us all, and the quest that he proposes? There is a risk involved in any such journey, because as Christ was confronted by the devil in the wilderness, so we will be tempted to undertake the journey just for ourselves – to save myself, to make my life better or more bearable, to improve myself, (how to win friends and influence people; you too can have a body like mine; how to become an authentic person in four easy stages) – and the ego will be only too pleased to take charge of the whole journey, making sure that the basic premise is 'What can *I* get out of this? What's in it for me?' But what we are seeking is the birth of the true self, not the enlargement of the great *I am*, or a sort of spiritual body-building course.

And the starting-point of the quest is self-love; accepting that God, existence, Being are to be trusted and that there is acceptance there for me as for all beings – acceptance, compassion and charity. Until we take ourselves seriously, accept that we have a moral obligation to ourselves, learn to accept ourselves completely, including the wounded, broken, disgusting, perverse, sick and hurtful parts, we will be powerless. Having no compassion for ourselves, how will we have it for others unless they fit our book of rules? Like the cross we must be firmly grounded, in touch with our roots, before we can support the weight of our open arms. But just as the four arms of the cross stretch out in different directions, so there will be conflict and tension in us too. How we long to follow a single straight path, to have only one meaning; for although we are a unity, we are a unity made up of contradictions and ambiguity. To start the journey is to accept that the paradox is an essential feature of human existence – we have to accept it, and live with it. How galling for our egos and our pride!

In a sense, all the Christian paradoxes revolve around an attitude of trust in existence. If we are terrified to make mistakes or risk failure we will never learn or grow, just as a child will never learn to walk without risking falling over and bumping into things. But we *are* frightened of making mistakes, we *are* frightened of being hurt. We build up massive defences, mental and material, because life strikes us as being basically hostile. The Christian paradoxes tell us that we have to unlearn all our precious defence mechanisms, because the only way ever to receive anything from life is to risk living in openness to Being; and we will fall, of course, and make mistakes, and be hurt, and yet real life is there at the end of it all.

When we have overcome our hoarding instinct, our empire-building instinct, our 'what's in it for me?' instinct, our 'it's better to be safe than sorry' instinct, and have dared to start on the road of openness to life, maybe we will learn that we were the prisoners of our own fear and that, by protecting ourselves from being hurt, we were walling ourselves in from life. As Jung wrote:

> When one lives one's own life, one must take mistakes into the bargain; life would not be complete without them. There is no guarantee – not for a single moment – that we will not fall into error or stumble into deadly peril. We may think there is a safe road, but that would be the road to death. Then nothing happens any longer – at any rate, not the right things. Anyone who takes the safe road is as good as dead.

So the road of love is really the road of freedom; freedom from the tyranny of self and all it feels it needs to protect or extend itself; freedom to confront life in the service of love and to discover one's true nature. It can be humiliating and painful to find out who one *really* is, but part of the journey is learning to accept all those aspects we'd like to keep locked away, saying, 'This too, is a part of me.' That doesn't mean that we then rush out and start indulging that part, simply that we accept that it is there, one of the many facets that go to make up the individual who is loved, accepted and *matters*.

If we accept ourselves fully, then we can start to love and serve others without condition. We no longer need to *demand* their love and acceptance, because we know we have a place in the order of things. Instead of protecting ourselves or groping for support and affirmation, we can give ourselves, because love is a going-out, an openness. Down come the walls of self-protection and all the things and people we thought we needed to give us a sense of worth or identity. By sticking to our quest, to the challenge and promise that the life of Christ offers us, perhaps we will give others the courage to face themselves, not cosseting them but helping them to find their unique meaning, and not condemning in them the things we have been unable to accept in ourselves.

Such openness and unconditional love and service for others, such obedience to the call of Christ, involves the death of dreams of power and happiness and security. It means that one has to follow a long, lonely and risky road, and yet that is the road where meaning is to be found.

> What is it, in the end (asks Jung), that induces a man to go his own way and to rise out of unconscious identity with the mass as out of a swathing mist? . . . It is what is commonly called *vocation*: an irrational factor that induces a man to emancipate himself from the herd and from its well-worn paths . . . Vocation acts like a law of God from which there is no escape . . . Anyone with a vocation hears the voice of the inner man: he is *called*. . . Unless one accepts one's fate . . . there is no individualisation; one remains a mere accident, a mortal nothing.

The cross calls us to find our meaning, to surrender all our childish longing for omnipotence and security, to take the risk of accepting ourselves, to bring that love and acceptance to all around us, and then to dare to believe that on the far side of the cross is a new birth. 'To be a Christian,' wrote Dietrich Bonhoeffer, 'does not mean to be religious in a particular way . . . but to be a man. It is not the religious act that makes the Christian, but participation in the sufferings of God in the secular life.' Or, as St Paul put it, we have been entrusted with God's work of reconciliation, breaking down the barriers that separate man from himself, and man from man, and man from God.

The cross is the death of that far distant God, uninvolved and watching, the death of living life for oneself, manipulating the world for comfort and security. The cross is suffering, Being-itself sharing in the struggle of human existence and agony; Being involved in all of life, not locked up in some religious cul-de-sac; the suffering of Christ who dared to show the way of self-offering; the suffering that is almost inevitable if we dare to be real and to follow him. The cross is the endless tension of meaning versus meaninglessness, with mankind stretched out in the middle. The cross is hope. After the torment, the struggle and the death comes – what? Not what we expected. Not what the world expects. The women run in terror from the empty tomb. Is love and meaning the victor after all? Can it really be true that good is indestructible?

5.   With friends like this . . .

No matter how much I may write about the power of love, about people like Viktor Frankl and Martin Luther King, or, going further afield, about the influence of someone like Gandhi, I don't think that the resurrection and the cross are concepts that can possibly make sense until they become more than concepts – until one has actually experienced them in oneself or in another person. So Lawrence Durrell has said about Yehudi Menuhin that he 'never fails to nudge each one of us with the reminder that goodness, if practised enough, could become contagious'. It may sound sacrilegious to some, but the fact or otherwise of Christ's resurrection purely as an incident in history seems as meaningless and as distant as the God 'out there', unless it is also a reality *now*, something vital and living that affects my life. For a man to be raised from the dead two thousand years ago in a strange land is just a freak, a miracle of resuscitation that I can't prove – something that may well distract me from confronting all that is dead and deathly in my own life. But to experience the birth of hope and new life in oneself or to witness it in another, *then* it can make sense, *then* some of the pieces start falling into place.

It is a dangerously circular argument. In a sense I am saying that you can't prove or disprove resurrection, just as you can't prove or disprove the existence of something called God: you can only experience it, or not. The one thing we can't have is certainty. Perhaps it's right that we should be cautious; Mark's gospel warned us about easy solutions and so, in their way, do Matthew, Luke and the authors of the 'happy' ending to Mark. Matthew reports, at the triumphant conclusion to his gospel, that when confronted by the risen Lord 'they fell prostrate, *though some were doubtful*'. Even the 'happy' ending of Mark says of those told about resurrection experiences, 'they did not believe it', 'no one believed'. Luke says that the disciples, on meeting the risen Christ, were 'startled and terrified, and thought they were seeing a ghost. . . they were still unconvinced, still wondering, for it seemed too good to be true'.

John's gospel confronts the problem of believing in the unbelievable through the story of Doubting Thomas, who refuses to believe the other disciples when they claim to have met the risen Lord. Thomas in turn is confronted by Jesus, who tells him to put his finger into the holes driven into his wrists by the nails. But Thomas doesn't touch Jesus; instead he makes a confession of faith. It is as if John is saying that Thomas is in the same position as the average Christian. He has not seen the risen Jesus and yet he is asked to believe. When confronted by Christ, and asked to touch him, what would he actually be believing in? A freak, a miracle? Thomas goes beyond that to say, 'My Lord, and My God', and such belief does not come merely from seeing ('some were doubtful'), but is a gift of God. We're back to circular arguments, and this is a particularly cruel one because it says that belief in God is a gift from God; you have either been given it or you haven't.

No wonder many people feel as if they have been refused admission to an exclusive club. They might like to join, but they haven't had an invitation from the chairman. But there's another resurrection story which moves in a different direction, and perhaps comes closer to all we've been saying about religion as a way of being, a journey, rather than a way of standing where you are, gritting your teeth and saying 'I believe.'

Two disillusioned, defeated disciples are walking to Emmaus. Christ has been crucified, and as far as they are concerned the show is over, ending in disaster and tragedy. A third man joins them on their journey and they talk together about all that has happened. At evening they reach the end of their journey. They ask the stranger to stay with them and have dinner. The man breaks bread with them and blesses it, and it is only then that they realise that their companion is Jesus, only then that, looking back, they can say, 'Did we not feel our hearts on fire as he talked with us on the road?'

Modern disciples face the same doubting, questioning road. Often our journey starts from some great defeat whose pain and loss we bring with us on the road. But we are not alone. There is someone with us, probing, questioning, challenging, encouraging. Who that companion is, we cannot fully understand or know until our journey is completed and night comes. What matters is to make the journey: 'You would not seek me if you had not found me.'

I have said that we can't begin to understand what resurrection means unless we have experienced it in ourselves, or in another. The Church is called 'the body of Christ' and if Christ is our companion on the journey, then it is the Church which should be helping us on our way, the Church as the body of Christ which brings us new life and has the power to burst open the tomb of our deadly lives. There are many ifs and buts and qualifications to what has to be said now, and we shall be trying to piece it all together in the next chapter. It may be hard to look at what I have just said without a deep sense of tragedy or, more likely, a loud and bitter laugh. The widow said that God is good for nothing and we have looked at some of the senses in which that is true. She also said that the Church is good for nothing. Let's not mince words, or my chances of future employment; what she actually said was, 'Fuck the Church,' and I'd like to try and explain why her words struck such a deep chord in me, reverberating more strongly with every passing year; why my answer to her is Hallelujah! Amen.

Part of her reaction was probably the natural and healthy expression of the deep anger that bereavement or loss can cause. (I hope that doesn't sound patronising, as if I were a doctor charting up symptoms.) Part of the anger was with God, the system or whoever had done this to her; the sort of feeling that you might find expressed by Stendhal more calmly and more cynically – 'God's only excuse is that he does not exist' – or by Woody Allen in one of his movies where he says something like' 'I don't think you could call God actually *evil*; perhaps the most you could say is that he's an under-achiever.' But I think that most of her anger came from the fear that the sudden pietistic note introduced by her friend meant that she was going to be denied what was most real to her at that moment; that the friend and I would gang up on her to cover up her wound with a lace handkerchief, rather than leave it to bleed freely and heal in its own time. In other words, that we would ignore the human factor and introduce some irrelevant and untimely fantasy.

This is exactly why Feuerbach found religion so deadly – literally deadly, anti-life, rather than deadly dull, although goodness knows both often apply. He said that God was just a projection of man's ideals and that a split had taken place – we keep all the muck and guilt, and project all the beauty of humanity on to something that doesn't exist. The danger of this is that religion directs all man's efforts into the pursuit and worship of the unreachable, and ignores the real truth – humanity. If there is to be hope for mankind, if wounds are to be healed, then we must 'transform theologians into anthropologists, lovers of God into lovers of man, candidates for the next world into students of this world, religious and political flunkeys of heavenly and earthly monarchs and lords into free, self-reliant citizens of the earth'.

We must add Feuerbach's warnings to Freud's, because both alert us to the dangerous distraction of the God 'out there' who keeps us safely childish and prevents us living as mankind come-of-age. And yet that is not the God we have been looking at on the cross, not the God that Bonhoeffer said 'is teaching us that we must live as men who can get along very well without him', not the God that Jesus incarnated, confronting people with the challenge and responsibility of their own existence. I become schizophrenic here, because I think there are two Churches. There is one, the real body of Christ, which continues as he did, powerless and loving. To be confronted by that is to be confronted by the spirit of Jesus; it's the Church that we shall be looking at in the next chapter.

But there is another Church, perhaps the one we're most familiar with, which seems specifically organised and maintained to live by everything that Feuerbach and Freud warned us about. And here we must add Durkheim's name to our list of critics, for Durkheim saw religion as a purely sociological phenomenon, as the way you express how you feel about your country, your position in society and so on. Through religious ritual you reaffirm your identity and values. Remembering a service at an English church somewhere in Europe – no names, I may want to go back some day – where the expatriate congregation, plus a few English tourists, yawned and sweltered their way through Holy Communion and then sprang to life to give a rousing, ram-rod-straight rendition of God Save the Queen, I can see what he meant. Or looking at those huge, empty Victorian churches in industrial towns, built by the management to keep the workers off the streets and suitably submissive on Sundays, or the whole tragic 'religious' situation in Northern Ireland, where a Christian nun could tell me that Mountbatten *deserved* to be murdered because, 'How dare he fly the Union Jack in Eire?'.

If we ask why people don't believe, when God is to do with a longing at the very centre of our lives, and why resurrection sounds so far-fetched and daydreamy, then I think we need look no further than the Church – the so-called body of Christ, but actually just another vast, depersonalising institution in a world full of vast, depersonalising institutions.

In *Little Dorrit* Dickens describes the most important government ministry, the Circumlocution Office, which exists to prevent anything of any importance happening – '*How not to do it*'.

> The Circumlocution Office went on mechanically, every day, keeping this wonderful, all-sufficient wheel of statesmanship, How not to do it, in motion. Because the Circumlocution Office was down upon any ill-advised public servant who was going to do it, or who appeared to be by any surprising accident in remote danger of doing it, with a minute, and a memorandum, and a letter of instructions, that extinguished him.

Although it's a comic vision, it's also a frightening one, because Dickens sees the whole of society as a monolith built to resist change and undermine all attempts at warmth, action or creativeness. Throughout the novel the image of the prison keeps recurring – restricting, threatening and destroying human values.

When I said in the prologue that religious bookshops sometimes make me want to behave like a guttersnipe, it's because they overwhelm me with a feeling of unreality. There they sit, and although they are dedicated to Christ and the love that bursts down the barriers that separate man from man, yet the prevailing feeling is one of death, of an institution devoted to keeping out anything contaminating to do with real people or real life. If human values are to be allowed in, then they have to be percolated through a very strong filter labelled 'Christian'. We have said that people are afraid of freedom, afraid of taking responsibility for their own lives. The Church can become the prison in which they willingly incarcerate themselves, surrendering their freedom to the warders, who also feel much safer living in a fixed institutional role and leaving the direction of their lives to the governor. Or perhaps the Church is the Ministry of Circumlocution, dedicated entirely to maintaining its own existence, providing limitless bumf within a totally self-enclosed environment. And if you think that's far-fetched, try talking to anyone who has been had up before the Sacred Congregation for the Faith in Rome, or who has crossed swords with their friendly neighbourhood bishop or a committee of dedicated 'Christians', or been condemned to a life of fund-raising.

But where does Jesus fit into all this? Well, technically, at the top – he is the head of the Church. But more often than not, the Church seems to have decided that he's an absentee landlord and the *real* power is given to popes, bishops, cardinals, synods, committees, civil servants, archdeacons, vicars, circuit superintendents, or what-have-you. And it's a power that comes across in very worldly terms; these are the head guys, the decision-makers, the deputy prison governors. You can live with this up to a point - if you accept that the Church must be institutionalised or organised to a certain extent if it's not to fragment into myriad individual pieces, for the functionaries then become necessary evils, keeping the show on the road. The problem starts when they are invested with mystic powers, and when they start to usurp the authority that should belong to each individual and, above all, to Christ. As we have seen, freedom causes anxiety, so we willingly hand it over, and then we start glamorising our loss of freedom by saying that it's a divinely ordained hierarchy that we are conforming to. Power belongs to the officer class – it's a safe, feudal system with a maximum of directedness, where everyone knows his place.

But in what direction are we heading? Surely the Church is simply a means to an end, not an end in itself? It is here to serve, to incarnate the powerlessness and suffering of God in the world, to convey the continuing challenge and promise of Christ. That means that *all* Christians have a ministry, *all* are priests, to use the old terminology, and the only time you find the idea of priesthood in the New Testament, apart from the final and perfect priesthood of Christ, is in the sense that *all* Christians are priests. It also means that there is only one absolute imperative for the Church: *it is here to fulfil its mission*. And all the hierarchies, ministries and structures are purely functional and must be judged and used in that light. Not 'how not to do it', but *'how to do it'*.

The hierarchical system that we are lumbered with at the moment owes far more to the structures of ancient Roman society than to the gospel; we even dress in the imperial purple. And the system was formed on strong neo-Platonic lines, based on the idea of the great chain of being, with God at the top of a sort of heavenly stairway, his power descending through neatly ordered ranks down to the bottom-most rung. Me priest; him deacon; you layman.

Well, all right, it's all very comforting, rather like the secure and ordered life of the services: you know where you are, and 'I was only obeying orders.' I know a parish where perfectly able-bodied and intelligent people all refer to the vicar, behind his back, as 'Sir'. Quite capable of running busy private and business lives, they surrender all responsibility to him in Church matters and become like children round a (loving) parent. But if Jesus is the head of the Church, shouldn't we stop and look at what sort of authority *he* practised and preached? The Church pays lip service to this, usually by saying that it's all right to be extremely important as long as you are also extremely humble. But

Jesus spoke about a new vision of authority that works exactly contrary to all our accepted and paternalism-loving ideas. What the gospels tell us quite specifically about Church authority is this:

> You know that in the world the recognised rulers lord it over their subjects, and their great men make them feel the weight of authority. That is not the way with you; among you, whoever wants to be great must be your servant, and whoever wants to be first must be the willing slave of all. For even the Son of Man did not come to be served but to serve, and to surrender his life as a ransom for many. [Mark 10:42]

> If anyone wants to be first, he must make himself last of all and the servant of all. [Mark 9:35]

> The highest among you must bear himself like the youngest, the chief of you like a servant. For who is greater – the one who sits at table or the servant who waits on him? Surely the one who sits at table. Yet here am I among you like a servant. [Luke 22:24]

> The least among you all – he is the greatest. [Luke 9:48]

> Happy are those servants whom the master finds on the alert when he comes. I tell you this: he will buckle his belt, seat them at table, and come and wait on them. [Luke 12:37 – the Master is God or Jesus; this is Luke's vision of what authority will be in the kingdom]

> The greatest among you must be your servant. For whoever exalts himself will be humbled; and whoever humbles himself will be exalted. [Matthew 23:11]

> The arrogant of heart and mind he has put to rout, he has torn imperial powers from their thrones, but the humble have been lifted high. The hungry he has satisfied with good things, the rich sent empty away. [Luke 1:51]

In John's gospel, at the Last Supper, Jesus gets down on his hands and knees and washes the disciples' feet. This was the job of the slave, or, occasionally, what a disciple might do for his rabbi; Jesus is their master and rabbi but he becomes their slave or disciple. 'If I, your Lord and Master, have washed your feet, you also ought to wash one another's feet. I have set you an example: you are to do as I have done for you' (John 13:14).

Jesus said quite specifically that Christian authority must be a hundred per cent different from that of the world – it is the authority of the servant, not of the leader. St Paul backs this up, basing his argument on the nature of Christ himself:

> There must be no competition among you, no conceit; but everybody is to be self-effacing. Always consider the other person to be better than yourself, so that nobody thinks of his own interests first but everybody thinks of other people's interests instead. In your mind you must be the same as Christ Jesus: His state was divine, yet he did not cling to his equality with God but emptied himself to assume the condition of a slave, and became as men are; and being as all men are, he was humbler yet, even to accepting death, death on a cross. [Phil.2:3-8]

However little the man in the street may know about Jesus, he knows at least the story of him dying for love and for others: if nothing else, the cross says something about giving up everything for the sake of other people (however mistakenly or unhistorically). And perhaps people see TV clips about Mother Teresa of Calcutta, or perhaps they have come across a real servant-priest, run down and worn out with quietly getting on with the business of loving and serving *all* the people in his parish (not just the Christians), not asking, just giving; and if so, then they may well be on the way to understanding what Christian love and service means.

But, it is all very quiet, unspoken; they may not even be conscious of it. There are other messages, other stimuli to catch the eye and perhaps to persuade them that this is what Christianity is *really* about. For instance, they may turn on the TV and, before switching over to something more interesting, get a glimpse of a figure dressed up like a Barbie doll with jewels and golden crosses and purple dress and cloth-of-gold cloak – Diana Dors? Danny La Rue? No, a Christian servant. (Obviously, servanthood is an attitude of the heart, not a matter of externals, but you need to have it written on your heart very deeply for it to make any headway through all the tat. I think that is why Cardinal Hume makes such an impact: even when loaded down with all the trappings of empire, the fact that he is a servant, not a lord, still shines through.)

Or supposing you are in love with a divorced man, and you both desperately want to marry in the sight of God, so you go to the local vicar (or servant) and he tells you that you are no better than a prostitute. This is a servant speaking? (It may sound far-fetched, but it's true – the woman was my mother.) Or supposing you're the woman who has just been told that she's dying of cancer and who goes to her vicar (or servant) for help, and he tells you that you must have committed some terrible sin for which you are being punished. (Also a true story, God help us.) These are all extreme cases, I know, but the attitude behind them is one that you find so often in the Church: lordship, judgeship, leadership – no sign of the servant.

Of course, Jesus' sort of authority is very challenging, because it passes the buck firmly back to us. Experiments have proved how easily we relinquish personal responsibility in a group or when with an authority figure; perhaps you have read about the instances of people being asked (as they thought) to torture a man as a scientific experiment under the authority of a dominant scientist: they found it extremely difficult to stop obeying orders – 'Turn up the electric current' – and follow their own sense of moral outrage. In another experiment an actor would pretend to have a fatal fit in a waiting-room with first one and then up to about fifty people. The fewer the people, the more instantaneous the reaction to help. When the crowd in the room reached a certain number, *nobody moved*. A secular style of authority in the Church appeals to our desire not to accept responsibility. What freedom we keep is safely channelled through Church institutions under the benevolent, paternal eye of the clergy.

In Kafka's *The Trial*, Joseph is harangued by a priest standing in a high pulpit. They are both alone in a vast, echoing cathedral, and the priest is yelling. 'If you want to talk to me,' says Joseph, 'come down and sit here in the pew beside me.' 'Oh, I dare not do that,' the priest replies, 'I have to speak to you at a distance, otherwise I am too easily influenced and tend to forget my duty.' By a secret, un-spoken conspiracy, we prefer the clergy, bishops and the rest to be authority figures because that eases the pain of accepting responsibility for our own lives. By the same token, the clergy condone this, because it gives them a safe and specific role to fill. And we like our authority figures to look and sound good. When I protested once about a particularly lordly prelate, someone said, 'Oh no, it's impor-tant for the Church to have good figureheads that we can look up to, and outsiders respect.'

But a Christian figurehead should be on his knees washing feet. Our real figurehead is a crucified, defeated Jew. St Paul was evidently a most unimpressive man, with some deep personal problem that he called his 'thorn in the flesh'. Moses had a speech impediment and had been in the desert for forty years. So where are the servants? Well, unnoticed obviously, that's their trademark. Being worldly-wise we know that a big organisation needs attractive logos and a good officer class. But if we think about the Church as it makes itself evident, does this ring a warning bell?

> They . . . wear deep fringes on their robes; they like to have places of honour at feasts and the chief seats in synagogues [churches?], to be greeted respectfully in the street, and to be addressed as 'rabbi' [Your Holiness, Your Grace, Father, Reverend, Minister . . .]. But you must not be called 'rabbi' for you have one Rabbi and you are all brothers. Do not call any man on earth 'father'; for you have one Father, and he is in heaven. Nor must you be called 'teacher'; for you have one Teacher, the Mes-siah. [Matthew 23:5]

We are back to the old question of who is really in charge – Jesus and the mission of the Church, or the Church itself, a large and circumlocutory organisation? If you look at the New Testament and early Church history you can't even defend the current system on divinely ordained grounds. As far as we know, Jesus didn't institute a specific ministerial class, and you can't trace the popes back to Peter except through legend. The office of presiding minister came about functionally, as the Eucharist became the main form of worship – you can't *all* break the bread – and the Church simply adopted the Jewish model of the sacrificing priest. The hierarchy came about because the Church was functioning in a highly structured, stratified society, and the original roles of prophet, presbyter, deacon, apostle, teacher, leader and bishop, which started as equal and, in some cases, interchangeable, gradually got involved in a power struggle, where some died out and some rose to the top, mimicking Roman power structures. And the whole thrust of this was to privatise the work of the Holy Spirit. Suddenly the Spirit of God which created all things and is instinct in all things, was nobbled and hemmed in by rules and regulations, so that the operation of the Spirit seemed now to depend on rites and hierarchic, hieratic modes, dangerously close to magic. And God/Being, this mysterious and wonderful surge of life, challenging, sustaining, creating, became the property of an exclusive few, locked up in a box, hemmed in by a holy huddle.

It would be tragic if it weren't so silly; Christians feel they must protect this poor little God and dole him out to suitable applicants. In Mark's gospel, Jesus says, 'He who is not against us is on our side' – in other words, they don't have to be Christians for the Spirit of God to be at work in them. The only important criterion is whether or not you are on the side of life. Dear old Matthew must have nearly swallowed his teeth when he was rewriting Mark and hit that one. So what does Matthew change it to? 'He who is not with me is against me' . . . If you're not in the team, forget it.

If the Church *has* gone wrong, if people outside it find it anti-life, could it be because we aren't following Jesus' basic instructions? Being a servant, humility, sacrifice, aren't just pious ideas: they are central, irreplaceable parts of the gospel and the mission of the Church. If we ignore them, we are turning our backs on the rule of God and setting up the rule of the Church and its officers. How prestigious, but how deeply anti-christ.

And what of the cross, all we've said about a God of weakness and about the Church providing a channel for his suffering presence in the world? Not a comfortable God to work for, so it's no surprise that Matthew's gospel, with its emphasis on order and discipline and its dislike of mystery, has tended to be the Church's favourite gospel. And when we don't want freedom or responsibility, how much nicer to have a big butch God out there, full of majesty and power, which his underlings then duplicate. Instead of each of us being called to follow that lonely and desperately hard Calvary road, the Church lays a nice bright six-lane highway, and we are all looking for the trappings of success – anything to prove that the absentee landlord still has power, that the organisation is successful. A nice full church, lots of conversions, coming across well on TV or radio, making a good impression as a super going concern full of super people, proving something to ourselves by speaking in 'tongues' - the list is endless.

But does a crucified man have anything to do with success, prestige or popularity? 'The figure of the crucified invalidates all thought which takes success as its standard,' wrote Bonhoeffer; *invalidates* – the whole thing becomes a ghastly sham because the Church has become a retreat from reality, dealing with cheap reassurance, rather than the body of Christ which plunges itself into human life, suffering, living, dying for others. 'I shrink to give up my life,' said Rabindranath Tagore, 'and thus do not plunge into the great waters of life'; the Church sits on the edge, nervously dabbling its toes in the water, and if you want to join it then you have to come out and dry yourself with a holy towel.

Jesus now has many lovers of his heavenly kingdom, but few bearers of his cross [wrote Thomas à Kempis].He hath many desirous of consolation but few of tribulation. He findeth many companions of His table, but few of His abstinence. All desire to rejoice with Him, few are willing to endure anything for Him, or with Him. Many follow Jesus unto the breaking of the bread, but few to the drinking of the cup of His passion. Many reverence His miracles, few follow the ignominy of His Cross.

It is the cross-bearers, the failed, the broken, the empty, unlovely, unprestigious, unglamorous, who are the real body of Christ. No resurrection without crucifixion, no life without death first – the Christian paradoxes at the heart of the gospel – but we are terrified to put them into practice because in our heart of hearts we believe that the folly of the cross *is* folly; we pay lip service to it, but never dare light the blue touch-paper.

Jesus didn't call us to be servants just as a nice but basically impractical idea. There was method in his madness, and surely part of it is to do with the Church, rather than aping and duplicating worldly power structures and systems, actually standing as a sign of contradiction to those systems. Our lives seem ruled by vast, impersonal forces – the state, the employer, multinational corporations, international power games; there is no one to say for the individual, 'Attention, attention must be finally paid to such a person.' But that is what the Church should be doing: it should be saying quite clearly and specifically to *every* person it meets, 'I am your servant', and it should be confronting all those power systems with its own position as the complete anti-thesis to all they stand for. The world demands that we take our places in the hierarchy and measure ourselves by our place in it; success and happiness depend on being able to climb or, at least, to hold our own. And the world tells us that we must succeed in order to be happy or acceptable. But unless you believe that the most important things in life are material possessions or the admiration of others, where do the most precious things in life fit into this scale? Where is real life to be found?

What is also worrying is the creeping gentrification to which the Church seems so prone, becoming a vast middle-class morass with aristocratic pretensions and making non-sense of any talk of foot-washing or the call to service. Why are the poor bishops always rolled out for aristocrats' weddings, baptisms or funerals, to lunch with the Queen, to dine with lord mayors or speak in the House of Lords? Why must Christian spokesmen always be so in line with The System, when the Church is not here to pat the establish-ment on the back, but to galvanise it into repentance.

Doesn't the cross give us a totally different image of what a Christian figurehead should be? 'He had no beauty, no majesty to draw our eyes, no grace to make us delight in him . . . He was despised, he shrank from the sight of men, tormented and humbled by suffering – we despised him, we held him of no account, a thing from which men turn away their eyes . . . ' (Isaiah 53).

At its worst, the Church is just a society within society, duplicating all its power and class systems, a bourgeois retirement home peddling paternalistic reassurance, folk religion and magic and ignoring the call to follow a betrayed and defeated Jew in incarnating God's suffering love in the world. No wonder the ex-Roman Catholic priest Charles Davis could say, after leaving the Church, that he felt 'as if I had rejoined the human race'. No wonder people look elsewhere to find a friend to help them on their journey. But if you actually dare to approach the Church, rather than laugh it off, how does it come across, can it help you on your way?

I sat in a lecture hall at Harvard University, packed with bright young American students and graduates. They were all there in the hope of finding some sort of answer to the deepest question of their lives, to the final question, as my companion put it, of 'What the **** is this mess all about?' Presently, a middle-aged ex-hero of the radical left got up on stage and began telling us of the transformation of his life by his belief in a young Indian guru who claimed to be Jesus, Buddha and Mohammed all in one, returned with more power and the ultimate solution. The audience was rapt. Although only a tentative Christian at the time, I watched their eagerness (and gullibility) with a feeling of horror and sadness – horror for the confidence trick being played on them, deep sadness for the fact that the Church seemed to have been quite unable to speak to their longing for meaning and direction: Christianity had nothing to say to them.

In one of his lectures at Columbia University, Bertrand Russell said that despite the complexities of the world's problems, our most urgent need is not for some new invention or technique but for something much simpler:

'The root of the matter is a very simple and old-fashioned thing, a thing so simple that I am almost ashamed to mention it, for fear of the derisive smile with which wise cynics will greet my words. The thing I mean – please forgive me for mentioning it – is love, Christian love, or compassion.' If those young Americans were right in their search for meaning: if Russell was right about the world's need for Christian love: if Christianity is, as I hope I've shown, at least a respectable intellectual option, a legitimate way of life, then what stops more people giving it a whirl? Why do people find it difficult to believe in the Christian story of God?

The answer is usually given in terms of death, child-suffering, cancer, the existence of evil and so on – 'How can I believe in a God who let my father die of cancer?' These are real enough objections, yet they don't stop other people from believing. Perhaps part of the answer lies in an African proverb: 'I cannot hear a word you are saying, because what you *are* shouts so loudly in my ears.' In other words, the real reason why so many seekers after truth can't believe in God, is the Church itself – the Church which says one thing but does another, which sometimes seems closer to being the Mother of Lies than the Bride of Christ – a huge mechanism for keeping people from the truth, for stopping them from being human.

Having experienced the Church from outside, as a non-believer, and from inside as an employee, I can well understand that for some people, asking the Church about the meaning of life would be like asking Hitler to recommend a kosher restaurant. This particular Hitler is a master of disguises, but if you peel them off you find that underneath he is characterised by a deep fear and dislike of people, unless they have been rigidly categorised (believer/ unbeliever, Catholic/Protestant, high/low church, sinner/ saint, and so on). I first came across this at Cambridge where, as an earnest inquirer after truth and being favourably disposed towards Christianity because of my family background, I put myself in the way of Christians in the hope that they might be able to help me in my search. My first discovery was that there were many different breeds of this strange animal and that instead of regarding me kindly, their immediate concern was to make sure that I hadn't been contaminated by contact with another breed. This done, they proceeded to explain at great length why I should avoid contact with the other breeds, why the other breeds were wrong/immoral/corrupt or just plain stupid, and why their breed was the only one that could help me.

Actually, 'help' is the wrong word, because I never at any time felt that anyone was interested in 'helping' me find the truth; they wanted to enrol me in their gang, and were prepared to use almost any means to indoctrinate me. There was the approach of probing one's life like a dentist looking for cavities and then, having found the nerve, pressing on it and saying, 'It hurts, but I can make it better'; there were the aggressive young men who cornered you at parties and demanded, 'Are you saved?' ('For this dance, honey, but I'll keep one for you later'); the élite dinner parties where silver-tongued monsignors from London made you feel how witty, elegant and upper-crust it would be; the parties and meetings where an escape was offered from the pressures of university life – are you lonely? Here we have instant friends; bewildered? Here we have instant answers; confused by this new, strange environment? We can cocoon you.

But it was security at a price: three untroubled years at Cambridge in a closed society, bought at the cost of surrendering the search for truth and meaning, and withdrawing from reality into a closed, bitchy little world. No wonder so many passionate student Christians drop the Christian lifebelt later – it has served its protective purpose. But this experience of Christianity at university was only symptomatic of the Church at large. 'Christian life,' wrote the Doctrine Commission of the Church of England, 'is an adventure, a voyage of discovery, a journey, sustained by faith and hope, towards a final and complete Communion with the Love at the heart of all things.' Hallelujah! But far from being an adventure or journey, the Christian life all too often seems to be put across as a gaining admission to, or being rabidly recruited by, a vast impersonal organisation, terrified of anything that might show cracks in the structure, and which seems to lay down rigid conditions of membership.

The first and most immediate condition seems to be that
you have to be good. If I had ten pence for every time I've
been told, 'Oh, I couldn't come into church, I'm not good
enough', I'd be living in sin in the Bahamas. The Church
gives the impression that people must be or behave in a
certain way before they can be acceptable. I shudder to
think what would happen in some churches if Jesus walked
in followed by his motley crew of whores, ex-whores,
extortionists, sinners (nature unspecified), party-goers,
fishermen, and the rest. The sort of middle-class morality
that masquerades as Christianity would make short work of
getting them *out*. Come to think of it, how would all those
peasant fishermen get on at Church selection conferences? –
No A levels, no public school tie, no Oxbridge theology
degree . . . whereas a Pharisee or chief priest would
probably have been able to muster excellent credentials.
This feeling that many people have that they are not
acceptable is something that hits you particularly strongly
when you get a dog collar round your neck. (There's an
opposite side to this too, of course, of dog-collars meaning
love and concern, due to the unsung devotion of countless
nameless priest-servants over the years.) When I first got
into clerical uniform it was a little like Frodo putting on the
ring of power in Tolkien's *The Lord of the Rings*. I entered
another world peopled by shadows and dark forces, while
the real world became hazy (suddenly jumble sales and
buildings and endless meetings became all-important, as
well as an unspoken desire to fill up the buildings with
people); the outside world, the world inhabited by the
majority of the population, became alien, of interest only as
a place to grab new recruits. Frodo's ring made him invisi-
ble; I sometimes felt, and still feel, something similar – the
collar becomes a screen on to which people project their
fantasies about clergy: father, brother, guru, fraud, and so
forth.

But the fantasy that I find most upsetting (and presumably
it is a fantasy that must have a toe-hold in truth, otherwise
how can so many people hold on to it for so long?) is the one
that assumes that the clergyman is going to *disapprove* – that
in some way you have to mask your usual, real behaviour

and personality, otherwise he is going to clobber you. Cigarettes are quietly stubbed out, drinks put down, language is modified or blushingly apologised for ('Damn – oh, I'm sorry, padre'), the divorced feel ashamed, couples living together try to hide the fact, gays keep it quiet. The list is endless, but the basic ingredient is the same: when confronted by a clergyman, people feel that in a central area of their life he is going to judge and/or reject them, that his acceptance and love are very strictly conditional – *eros*, not *agape*.

Even if people manage to evade the censors and join a church, how often do they feel that they have to keep certain areas of their lives secret, for fear of condemnation? Where has this ideal Christian sprung from, the barrister with perfect teeth, two children, charming wife, classless accent and no problems worth mentioning? How is Christ more in him than in his fellow barrister, hanging round the Charing Cross gents, frightened to go home to a loveless marriage?

The other condition of membership is the ability to swallow whole a vast body of propositions. Far from starting on a journey, being a Christian can seem more like signing one of those endless hire-purchase contracts, where you have to agree to an encyclopaedic list of conditions. Whosoever would be saved, or at any rate join the club, must believe X, Y, Z. There follows a mind-blowing list to which you may say 'Bollocks!', or you may gratefully accept it as truths from on high which will prevent you thinking or worrying. Or else, like many Christians, you manfully keep your doubts to yourself and lock your 'simple faith' and 'everyday life' into separate compartments, trustingly refusing to use on your faith the same questioning approach that you would apply to any other corner of your life, and wrestling with a growing sense of unease and discontent which you dimly feel may be sinful. Is it any wonder that, in church after church, you hear the confused appeal, 'Please can we have more teaching?' Teaching about what? Not sure, but something to ease the pain. Because of course the other thing we all know is that Christians *never feel doubt*, or if they do, they've got to keep it to themselves.

There are historical reasons why the Church got lumbered with its credal systems; it felt it had to get exactly what it stood for written down and solidified as soon as possible, under the pressure from all sorts of weird sects, pagans and heretics. For example, when people said that Jesus was so completely divine that he had no human feelings at all and just 'usefully pretended to suffer', the Church had to try to explain why that was wrong – and the easiest way to do that was to set out what it thought was right. Early theologians approached their task very tentatively – rightly – and with a sense that they were speaking about what was best left unspoken.

Anyone who has studied the early history of the Church and its theological struggles will tell you that it was an incredibly complex time, as they tried to hammer out the implications of all that had happened. The final solution, if solution it was, came about more through political pressure than actual agreement. The Emperor Constantine was horrified to discover that his new state religion of Christianity, far from being the uncomplicated worship of a God resembling the unconquered sun, had got all the theologians battling over issues even more complex and incomprehensible than an episode of *Crossroads* when you have missed the previous three. The solution they arrived at was a political compromise, but it forms the basis of the credal system we have inherited. More to the point, these creeds (based on compromise) and the Bible (that motley collection of books) are what people believe make up a Christian: to be Christian is to assent to facts (?) X, Y, Z. Unfortunately, the institution seems to go along with this, too. In church you have read to you with due solemnity how God orders some ancient Israelite to murder another tribe and take their land, then in the next breath you are told that God is love, and you are left to swallow the whole package. Likewise the creeds, Sunday after Sunday, as if assenting to them makes you a Christian.

The trouble is, as we have said, that the Church becomes an end in itself, not a means to an end, and once you've joined the organisation, that's it for the rest of your life – all you have to do is to keep attending regularly, keep repeating the passwords, keep taking the tablets . . . be a good organisation man (I won't say woman, because although women and the traditionally feminine virtues of nurturing, feeding, warming, holding, comforting and giving life, really make the backbone of the Church, the Church itself never really knows what to do with them: 'The only place for women in the Church is on their knees,' a young ordinand told me, 'scrubbing or praying'). And some people are content to remain good organisation men all their lives. The Church becomes like Noah's Ark – you climb inside where it's cosy and safe and where there's a captain to tell you what to do, and you close your eyes and your mind to the people outside, and you get on with ship's concerts, swabbing the deck, jumble sales, youth clubs, women's groups – anything to keep your mind off the big, nasty world outside.

This is all right for people who join the Church because they are frightened of the pain of growing and changing; but supposing you came to the organisation not for security or to become an organisation man, but to look for answers or to help you in your search – what sort of growth or enlightenment does such a trip offer you? No wonder some Christians feel dissatisfied and restless – they are being asked to worship the Church and its book of rules, not to seek for God. And no wonder other Christians strike you as dead from the heart up – they have run away from the pain and struggle of the search and sold their true identity for a mess of Mothers' Union potage.

The problem is that the starting-point for the search is often a dim awareness of the unhealed or wounded parts of the personality. When confronted by pain we react in the same way as we do to anxiety; we can either try to go back, or freeze where we are, or have the courage to struggle through the darkness. Research into 'happiness' or well-being has shown that it can never be found as an end in itself, but is always a by-product of something greater, just as self-realisation can never be an end in itself but comes only as a by-product of self-transcendence, the service of something greater. People at the crossroads of life, when confronted by crisis or tragedy or simply by a dim, unexpressed need, can either pass the buck by blaming others, or

their stars or fate or God; or they can join the living dead
(like that terrible epitaph, 'She died at thirty, and was buried
at seventy'; or they can take the risk of change and of finding
their own creative personal solution.

For some time I tried to excuse the deadness of many
Christians, and the outrageously childish and empire-
building behaviour of others, by saying that the Church was
bound to be full of human frailties simply because it is
human; Christians aren't saints. But I think the problem
goes deeper than that. People who come to the Church with
wounds need to be supported, but they also need to be given
the courage to face those wounds, to accept the unacceptable in themselves, to be given the strength to go on with
their journey. Similarly, people full of unresolved conflicts,
like the need to play power games or the inability to take
responsibility for their own lives and the desire to be
fathered, should be helped to grow beyond these phases.
But all too often the Church, instead of being the starting-
point for the individual's journey, where he is fed, watered
and encouraged, is seen as the terminus; a nursery where
you are given space to remain childish and unhealed and can
avoid all the pain and anxiety of growth. The reason why
some Christians seem deadly is that they *are* dead – the
Church has allowed (encouraged?) them to hide from the
pain of life on the condition that they remain loyal to the
organisation; their energies are diverted from growth and
reality towards keeping the organisation going.

Bette Midler describes meeting a desperately active
woman, full of wonderful schemes for things to do: 'I'd say
she was about thirty-five and had never been – or, having
been, was disappointed.' Perhaps we all know those incredibly busy Christians, buzzing with good works, once described as '[living] for others; you can tell the others by their
hunted looks'. Perhaps that's the secret – that all the
activity, all the good deeds, reveal a desperate need to evade
the vacuum inside themselves. And you can always tell
inside when someone helps you from genuine free love, or
when there are strings attached, such as the desire to prove
their own usefulness or to deny their deepest feelings of
being unlovable, unworthy, unwanted. In the same way

meditation, that stillness which can be the most searching, creative and painful of prayers, can also be a neurotic flight from action; the frightened child who freezes rather than dare move. And perhaps the reason why some of us seem unable to grow as people or as Christians is that our prayer life is used as a shield against the pressures of reality and an evasion of the questions that life (or God?) is asking us.

How else to explain the people who spend long hours in prayer and yet whose lives bear such bitter fruit for others? A wise nun once told me that the only way you could measure the 'success' or otherwise of your prayer life was by your increased capacity to suffer. But that's exactly what we don't want to do – we want to be holy, or to sense the presence of God, or get our prayers answered, not to suffer alongside Christ. And so as not to suffer the pain of becoming real, we concentrate our energies on the all-wonderful out-there, forgetting that true spirituality has to do with what John Macquarrie calls 'becoming a person in the fullest sense'. Or else we get involved in the power structures of the Church, building little empires for ourselves, from 'my pillar, where I *always* do the flowers' to 'my committee', 'my parish', 'my diocese', 'my Church'. But it's not *my* anything; Christ is the head of the Church, and we are all servants, and it is Christ's pillar, Christ's committee, Christ's parish, Christ's diocese, Christ's Church – the poor tired old tramp sitting outside the church being far more important than the visiting dignitary being paraded inside.

Madness? Nonsense? Possibly, but I can't help feeling that if we dared to take Jesus seriously and accept that, for example, that failed whisky-priest who has just scandalised his congregation by having a sad and desperate affair with the organist's wife may be *more* important and closer to the gospel than a sovereign pontiff being carried high amongst cheering thousands, then what painful and overdue growth into adulthood we might make. The man we follow is a broken, desolate failure, a man of sorrows and acquainted with grief, not a media-marvel, a natural leader, the kind of person people usually expect to look up to and admire. If Christians do have someone to look up to, it is because he is there above them, nailed powerless and broken to a cross.

But who can blame the layman for getting it wrong, when that is all the Church will offer him? He's only doing what he's told; only following the example of those potent stumbling-blocks to belief, the clergy. (Oh God, yes, of course, starting-blocks to belief, too, some of them, but how few, how rare.) I've already mentioned people's fear of the clergy condemning them, but I don't think that is the major obstacle to belief. The real problem is less easy to define but can perhaps be approached obliquely by describing Carl Rogers' theory of 'congruence'. Briefly, he says that no analyst, counsellor or therapist can possibly be of help to a client, unless the client senses that what he says and what he does are in harmony, that he too is striving towards wholeness of being. In the end it is the *person* of the counsellor that matters, not the techniques he uses.

A friend of mine was enjoying a meal in a motorway café which was packed with lively people. Suddenly conversations slowed down and died as two clergymen, dressed from head to foot in black like carrion crows, walked in; the joy vanished. Did the people in the café feel that there was something less than human about those two figures in black? What worries me about so many clergy is the feeling that somehow they're not quite real people, not quite believable. Sometimes they remind me of creatures from another planet who have closely studied human behaviour and now are trying to duplicate it, not altogether successfully.

For instance, some have obviously observed humans smiling and laughing and noticed that this has a good effect on other humans, so they have evolved a whole repertoire of teeth-baring smiles and hearty laughs, just to prove what fun it all is, how nice and deeply loving they are, what joy in the Lord if you enrol here; but the smiles and laughs are not for you where you are, loving and accepting you, comrades on the same journey: They are the smiles of the great white shark in *Jaws* who has spied another potential mouthful, another feather in the Lord's cap. Other clergy don't even bother to imitate human behaviour; they worship the icon of The Priest and probably have done so ever since they were little, and they have abdicated from the pain and struggle of becoming real by hiding behind the icon. The dog collar and cassock, the sacraments and prayers, the religious stance and 'Father knows', become sandbags from behind which frightened little boys snipe at anyone who isn't one of them, and keep at arm's length anything of real warmth and compassion.

Or there are the 'busy' clergy, always in a rush, always full of good works, always organising something new, something to bring the people in and then keep them amused once they've got them there; like the Red Queen in *Through the Looking Glass*, they run desperately in order to stay on the same spot, but if they ever stopped running, would there be anybody there?

Then there are the 'look at me' clergy, a fascinating breed from all denominations, whose behaviour and approach is always that bit larger than life; at clergy meetings they stand out with their dramatic gestures and actors' voices, trumpeting the latest success story; meanwhile their wives, timid and quiet and depressed, hover respectfully in the background. Or the bookish clergy, who almost smell of dust. If you display human needs or emotions, they look at you through their spectacles with frightened eyes. Their minds work in neat formulae, and humans worry them because they don't quite fit. They will teach, advise, admonish and direct you, but they will not love you or get involved because love is too untidy and risky – they might melt in the warmth. Unreal indeed, these two-dimensional people; they admonish us to believe and to perform acts of charity, and perhaps we try, but they cannot really feed us, cannot help us on our search, because they themselves have given up the search long ago and settled for a role to play and a book of rules to follow. Shall I ever forget the clergyman who confronted me once in the staff car park at the crematorium? I had just taken the particularly harrowing funeral of a young father of four, and I was crying. Enter the clergyman, bristling, all guns blazing, and spat at me, 'You ought to be *ashamed* of yourself!'

But it's not all their fault, either; how easy it is to get frozen into a professional role when you are confronted with so much suffering, so many pressures to play a part, and the Church doesn't seem to give a damn whether you live or die

as long as you aren't caught seducing the choir. If the
Church doesn't really know what clergy are for, except as
the paid professionals who have to motivate a voluntary
membership and keep roofs on decaying buildings, then how
are clergy supposed to know? At theological college would-
be priests are taught how to do a million different things,
from declining Greek verbs to giving old ladies bedpans. But
the great black-hole in the syllabus, invalidating all the
reams of academic and socially helpful instruction, is the
absence of soul, Being, suffering, humility. In the end,
priests have nothing to offer anyone except their reality, the
pain of their search, their struggle for growth and realisation, their courage and hope in staying true to the turmoil in
their souls – their wrestling with God. But there is no space
for wrestling with God on a college timetable, nor can you
pass exams in it. If people stay away from church, if they
despise the clergy, isn't it because they sense that these are
people who have abandoned the struggle and turned their
backs on the very questions that agonise so many? The
colleges go on churning out salesmen, junior officers, organisation men with their eyes fixed on the ladder; but
pilgrims, explorers, suffering servants, healers not afraid of
their own wounds – rarely, very rarely.

When I arrived at theological college straight from an
agnostic/humanist organisation dedicated to love and service, I couldn't believe the difference. There would be
discussions about moral cases, about what we'd do when we
'got into the parish', what advice we'd give, how we'd build
up the congregation . . . always what 'we'd do' – as if we
were the answer to every problem. Quite a lot of students
had come straight from school and university, never having
had to earn their living. If I wrote about the hatred and
savagery (called 'speaking the truth in love') that went on
there, no one would believe me. Many of the students
appeared to look on college as a rather unnecessary hurdle
between themselves and their opportunity to get out there as
A Clergyman. Like the goddess Athena they needed no
process of birth, having obviously sprung fully armed from
inside their fathers' heads.

And they *knew*, they were so confident, so sure – I'll do this, I'll do that, that's sinful, that all right – as they waited to be given power: power to bash Bibles, convert, grab, evangelise (but not power to love and be with people, to respect them as they are without wanting to make them in your own image, to cry with people and hurt when they hurt – oh no, 'I'll pray for you', that glib turn-off, but never 'I'll watch with you'); power to celebrate the mass, to forgive sins, to become mighty in prayer, to dress in different clothes, be treated with respect, called Father, have a unique and special role as guardian of the sacred mysteries (but not power to help themselves through the agony of becoming nothing, the lowest of the low, the servant of all, to help them in the greatest mystery of all, the way of the cross); or perhaps just power to be the key figure in an institution, to organise people, get their approval and admiration, direct, judge, reprove, approve, preach, teach, tell them where it's at, and hopefully in time, if you play your cards right, do it all in trumps from under a bishop's hat (but not power enough to admit 'I don't know', 'I thirst', 'I hurt', 'We travel a difficult unknown road together and I am your servant, not the traffic cop/magistrate/star of the show').

Power, status, position: I was at a meeting of clergy where an elderly priest stood up and said that he had been lost for forty years; for forty years he had been pretending to be something he wasn't. He came from a working-class background but on becoming a clergyman had also become middle-class in accent, attitudes, the way he expected to be treated (doctor, parson, lawyer – that level). The week before this clergy meeting someone had met him in the street and, instead of saying, 'Good morning, Father', had called out, 'Hello, Ted'. It was only then that he realised that the reason why he was depressed, run down and cynical was that for most of his life he had been playing a part and that Ted, the real him, had been locked away.

We are back to the question of why clergy seem unreal as people, and playing a part has a lot to do with it. Have you noticed, for example, the strange uniformity of accent amongst the clergy? If they haven't been through public

school, Oxbridge and the guards, after a year or so of
theological college the odds are that they will talk as if they
have. They are still trained and regarded (perhaps even, oh
save us, by themselves) as the Christian officer class, imbued
with what George Eliot called 'that frigid mincingness called
dignity, which some have thought a peculiar clerical disease'.

And why must they pretend to be perfect, holy, loving
gentlemen when their families and those who know them
closest are well aware that they aren't? It's convenient for
people to pretend that clergy are very holy and perfect
because it stops them having to bother to be holy themselves. The clergyman becomes the token saint because both
he and other people would find it very threatening if he
started developing human weaknesses and reactions; it
would involve painful growth on both sides: growth in
self-acceptance, and growth in loving acceptance, that is to
say, the unconditional acceptance of another. The outside
world knows what a lie this icon of the perfect man is; that's
why they delight so much in Sunday paper scandals about
vicars and prostitutes, drugs, choirboys, wife-swapping and
the like. There is something in the make-up of some clergy
that is deeply suspicious and fearful of humanity, either in
themselves or in other people. That's why you can find
gathered round a vicar whole congregations in that vicar's
own image, dull and grey and terrified of anything noisy and
mucky and human. George Orwell wrote:

> It is probable that some who achieve or aspire to saint-
> hood have never felt much temptation to be human beings
> . . . No doubt alcohol, tobacco and so forth are things that
> a saint must avoid, but sainthood is also a thing that
> human beings must avoid . . . in this yogi-ridden age, it is
> too readily assumed that 'non-attachment' is not only
> better than a full acceptance of earthly life, but that the
> ordinary man only rejects it because it is too difficult: in
> other words that the average human being is a failed saint.
> It is doubtful whether this is true . . . if one could follow it
> to its psychological roots, one would, I believe, find that
> the main motive for 'non-attachment' is a desire to escape

from the pain of living, and above all from love, which, sexual or non-sexual, is hard work.

That is the heart of the matter: that there is a false sanctity, to do with perfecting oneself and pursuing a distant God not to be found in oneself or other people; and there is the true sanctity, where the real saints belong, to do with being human, taking as one's cue the assertion that God became man because he loves man so much. Orwell again:

> The essence of being human is that one does not seek perfection, that one is sometimes willing to commit sins for the sake of loyalty, that one does not push asceticism to the point where it makes friendly intercourse impossible, and that one is prepared in the end to be defeated and broken up by life, which is the inevitable price of fastening one's love upon other human individuals.

But this is threatening and difficult because it's not black and white and it involves suffering, perplexity and growth.

Suffering, perplexity and growth – but these are aspects that are anathema to paternalism; and the Church, alas, as you would expect from an organisation that calls its servants 'Father', can be a sucker for paternalism. It starts at the very top with Daddy God, who tucks you up at night and promises that all will be well, and kisses you better when you cry; then there's Daddy Priest, who tells you what to do and, like all fathers, is supposed to be omnipresent, omnipotent, omniscient, omnicompetent and very, very good (and you'd better be good too or he'll spank you). This model works for one to five-year-olds, but humanity is slowly, painfully getting a bit older now, and when we stop to think about it we know that fathers can't possibly be omnipresent, omnipotent . . . and that there's no point in getting cross with them when they aren't. Indeed it's a great milestone for any individual when he or she makes the painful realisation that his or her parents aren't perfect but simply human like everyone else, and that instead of putting the onus of decision, moral judgement and behaviour on to them, we have to shoulder it for ourselves. When one can accept and love human weakness in one's parents, instead of secretly boiling because parents should be perfect, then surely adulthood cannot be far off. But it is very difficult to get that far; I think of a friend who arrived home unexpectedly to find his mother in bed with a strange man. Another melodramatic example? All right, then how do you react to the vicar who is having an affair with another woman, or who is an alcoholic, or gay, or having a nervous breakdown, or getting a divorce. The child says kill – get him out; the adult says, poor bastard, there, but for . . .

It makes life much easier for the Church if people are kept at the level of the child. They are more obedient, more respectful (status again!), they ask fewer questions, or rather, the questions they ask are less awkward. But for anyone who really loves humanity this paternalism is sickening, because it stunts people's growth; the Church becomes a never-never land full of lost boys and girls who refuse to grow up, led by a clerical Peter Pan who occasionally crows to himself as he watches his swelling congregation, 'Oh the cleverness of me' (but never out loud, because the congregation likes to know he's humble). Is this another reason why people who really love their fellow man feel sympathetic to Christ but worried by the Church? Perhaps they remember that it was the Pharisees, not Jesus, who insisted on rules and righteousness, the pursuit of self-perfection and outward rectitude; the Pharisees who rushed to condemn and throw the first stone, who played a very definite fixed role, replete with status, power and authority.

Jesus, on the other hand, is less easy to tie down; what did he *do*, exactly? Well, he was. He existed. He was real. Wherever humans went, he went – he didn't hang around the temple moaning to God about how awful they were or polishing his halo. Jesus cured and cared by being himself with people, not by playing a part. And in the end he challenged the world to search for the meaning of life by laying down his own for love, as a servant. He preached, wandered, visited, told stories, chatted, argued, drank, went on picnics and to dinner parties, touched, prayed, wept, doubted, suffered, agonised, died – he lived to the full his own destiny, true to God and to himself. And isn't *that* what clergy should be doing, refusing to play a part no matter how great the rewards in terms of approbation, status, cushioning, but rather struggling to be true, to follow the path of the servant, the way of the cross? And in doing so they are bound to get a lot of flak because they will be challenging people out of their preconceptions, challenging them to take responsibility for their own lives instead of eternally passing the buck, challenging them to grow up and start loving and serving people instead of weighing and measuring them.

If you know a servant-priest or servant-Christian, you may wonder what on earth I've been going on about, because you will have experienced with them something of what I tried to say in chapter 4 about the cross: you will know what it is to be accepted totally, no matter what. And if that's so, you won't give a toss about all the nonsense the Church gets up to, because you'll have discovered that the Church really is nonetheless the body of Christ – underneath all the layers of muck the work of love goes on, quietly, patiently, unheralded, just as it has done since the beginning.

And what happens when you're loved like that? In Margery Williams' book *The Velveteen Rabbit* a new toy rabbit arrives in the nursery and discovers that, although most of the toys, however posh, bright or glittery, are 'only toys, and would never turn into anything else', there is another toy, an old battered Skin Horse, who has become real.

'What is *real*?' asked the Rabbit one day, 'does it mean having things that buzz inside you and a stick-out handle?' 'Real isn't how you are made,' said the Skin Horse. 'It's a thing that happens to you. When a child loves you for a long, long time, not just to play with, but *really* loves you, then you become Real.' 'Does it hurt?' asked the Rabbit. 'Sometimes,' said the Skin Horse, for he was always truthful. 'When you are Real you don't mind being hurt.' 'Does it happen all at once, like being wound up,' he asked, 'or bit by bit?' 'It doesn't happen all at once,' said the Skin Horse. 'You become. It takes a long time. That's why it doesn't often happen to people who break easily, or have sharp edges, or who have to be carefully kept.

Generally, by the time you are Real, most of your hair has been loved off, and your eyes drop out and you get loose in the joints and very shabby. But these things don't matter at all, because once you are Real you can't be ugly, except to people who don't understand.'

The Rabbit sighed. He thought it would be a long time before this magic called Real happened to him. He longed to become Real, to know what it felt like; and yet the idea of growing shabby and losing his eyes and whiskers was rather sad. He wished that he could become it without these uncomfortable things happening to him.

If someone looking for the truth meets only the posh, bright, glittering mechanical toys of the Church, then who can blame them if they look elsewhere for reality? If they are lucky enough to meet a Christian who is Real, probably loose in the joints and very shabby, who knows what healing will be there? – whether they will suddenly understand that resurrection isn't a boring academic question about ancient history but something that is true now and always, the power of love that can burst through the tomb of our deadly lives.

Excursus

Once upon a time there was a faith-healer who travelled round the country curing people of various ills – coughs, colds, housemaid's knee, and so forth. But the great impact he made was more because of what he was than what he did: he taught people to look at themselves and other people in a new way, to find treasure in the most unlikely places. After he left the country, people tried to work out how he could have made such an impression, and over a period of years they worked out a formula for a potion that they hoped would duplicate his effect. This was duly marketed as Miracle Elixir and over the years it became stupendously successful. A vast management team was built up, stringent copyrights and patents were issued, enormous offices, factories, shops and exhibition halls sprang up, and highly motivated salesmen were sent everywhere to sell the stuff. But as the years went by people began to forget what the

Miracle Elixir was for: rival companies were set up using almost the same ingredients and claiming better effects.

Gradually, the public lost interest in the Miracle Elixir – and anyway it didn't seem to work so well as in the old days – but the company was too preoccupied with salesmanship and company traditions to ask itself what was going wrong. Instead they tried all sorts of gimmicks: exciting packaging, modernised instruction leaflet, testimonials from filmstars, musical bottles, singing salesmen, group discounts; they even extended the claims of the product by suggesting all sorts of new uses for it – cleaning carpets, washing hair, keeping teenagers off the streets, stopping girls getting pregnant. In fact, they tried everything they could think of to persuade people that the elixir could still be useful and fill a gap in their lives. What gap? Any gap! But sales still kept dropping and even the salesmen began to wonder if it was worth all the effort and if the Miracle Elixir really worked at all; some just got depressed, but conscientious ones swallowed their doubts, redoubled their efforts and gladly went on every salesmanship course and conference the company could devise.

But one day in the directors' board room, where some of them were old and some cynical and one or two of them, I'm afraid, were too busy enjoying the view from the top to have time even to taste the elixir, one day consternation reigned. The portrait of the founder, in top hat and tails, grasping in one hand a bottle of the elixir and in the other a copy of the formula, had been X-rayed before cleaning. Under the thick layers of paint and varnish and restoration by many different hands, the X-ray revealed the original painting – rather crude, but vivid. There, under the overpainting of centuries, was not the suave, attractive gentleman with bottle and prescription, friend of royalty, TV celebrities and cabinet ministers, but a wild-eyed tinker with a curiously disconcerting smile, holding out his empty hands as if to embrace the viewer, not sell something to him. There was no bottle, no prescription – just a look of love and challenge.

The directors were horrified – what should they do? Restore the picture to the original? Destroy the X-ray? Call twenty-four board meetings? And how would all this affect

sales? Can you have an organisation unless you are marketing something specific? Can you market a look in the eye?

6.   They also serve

I wanted to start this chapter in a measured and kindly way, saying that the Church is all right really; you only have to look closely to see that, despite all its faults, the spirit of Christ still rules and heals. But I have just come back to my desk after four hours with a desperate, desolate man; a lifetime Christian with a highly responsible job and unimaginable family problems, a kingpin in a vast multinational corporation, who cried in my arms because no one had ever told him before that he is *loved*: loved, unconditionally; accepted, totally; forgiven completely; important, beautiful, radiant with God's love burning in him . . . Yet his whole life is lived in a deep cloud of guilt and fear because his Christian training and background tell him that he has *failed* – failed to measure up to the test; *failed* to reach an acceptable standard; *failed* to be worthy of God's love.

I wanted to be measured and kindly, but I walked back through the streets of Paddington with all its thousands of human beings, each with his secret and desperately important life, saying to myself, 'What the hell are we doing? What is this cruel and savage god we perpetrate, this conditional love we dole out to acceptable applicants – this anti-Christ we preach?' All that talk of the need to love and accept ourselves, of the Church as a servant, the lowliest foot-washers, isn't just theory; it's the keystone of the whole Christian arch, without which the entire wretched structure tumbles to the ground.

No one has ever told that man that he matters, that he is loved, that God suffers in him instead of standing aloof and condemning. I had met him in the pub because he no longer goes to church; in the pub he meets other human beings who at least give him fellowship and friendship; in church he finds nothing but conditional acceptance. His pain, the wound that is the most real thing in his life at the moment, has to be kept hidden safely away. What are we doing? What, in God's name, are we doing?

Why is the Church, which should be the most human and accepting of all places, the most remote to the majority of people? Why do people say to me with such amazement, after a few minutes' conversation, 'But you seem so human'? Why do outsiders come for wedding interviews and such like in trepidation and on their best behaviour, as if they expected to be met by a headmaster or a hanging-judge rather than a loving servant? Have we become so bogged down in creeds and dogma that we have lost touch with real life, or is there a deeper problem?

Erich Fromm has written about paternal love as being quite different from maternal love: the mother accepts and cherishes, ideally creating a sense of affirmation not just of the child but of life itself – *life is good*! Mother's love also wants the child to grow, in the end, to be able to separate itself from her. The father, however, offers conditional approval; his respect and love must be earned.

If the bulk of the Church is made up of people who are unable to accept or have compassion for themselves, and who worship the Father out-there who – in total contrast to the true gospel – only gives love in return for good behaviour and correct attitudes, is it any wonder that the Church is unable to give anything to the world but paternal love, hedged in with conditions and codicils and sub-clauses? If we are to give you love, says the Church, then you must first deserve it. The unspoken message, of course, is that you are not lovable in yourself; you must *win* love by pleasing, owning, or doing. When treated like that, we realise in the end that we are not loved but *conned*. Perhaps that is why so many people I admire will have nothing to do with the Church; they have grown beyond the need to win approval or to be patted on the back. They know that life is a lonely journey and the Church is a total irrelevancy to them, denying as it does that the insights they have reached with such struggle can have any value unless they can be catego-rised as Christian. The hero on his journey has no need of umpires or uninvolved spectators; what he needs is a companion or a place of rest and refreshment on the way – not traffic lights and one-way systems, magistrates and parking fines.

So much depends on the image of God that the Church follows. What would Feuerbach have said to the man I met in the pub? That his whole Christian upbringing and training had taught him to disregard all that was good and true in his life, even the nobility of his suffering, to project it on to a far-distant, perfect deity and to keep for himself all the guilt and shame and failure so that he would live in a perpetual state of pain? Anyway, that's what has happened, and the man is frozen, unable to move on or grow because he feels that God is perfect, he is a failure, and the most the Church can do for him now is to give him conditional forgiveness and increase his sense of guilt. And perhaps Freud would add that he is being kept in a child-like state of needing and seeking Daddy's forgiveness and approval, when the truth is that he is caught up in a tragic situation not of his own making, where the fault, if fault there be, seems to me to lie very firmly at God's door. But what if the Church had told him about the God that we have been trying to look at in this book? Perhaps the time has come to look at the way the Church might behave when it is freed from the shackles about which Feuerbach, Durkheim and Freud warned us.

Surely, in such a Church, freedom is the most important element. If we *really* believe that God is Being-itself, the most substantial reality undergirding all creation, creating, sustaining, calling into fullness of being, then surely our most basic attitudes are of hope and trust. Being-itself is everywhere, instinct in everything, and that means our attitude to all creation should be one of care and openness. Christianity has always had a tendency towards dualism, towards saying that created things are basically bad, whereas the Creator is all good; pan-en-theism says that there is good in everything because God is to be found everywhere. That means that the Church, far from having its back to the wall and seeing itself as the one element of salvation in a dark and sinful world, can, on the contrary, afford to be free and flexible. It is not here to preserve itself or to fight off the pagan hordes, but to convey the continuing presence and ministry of Christ, calling the world to awareness of the good news, the vital unique importance of each individual human soul and personality, urging people to be aware of the presence of God, of Being, within themselves and within each other.

And if God, Being, meaning is everywhere, then it is quite certain that the other great religions have caught sight of it too, and instead of feeling threatened, as if it put the Christian insights at risk, surely we can rejoice at the breadth of its revelation. The early Church was certainly perfectly happy to incorporate into itself whatever it found in paganism that was compatible or adaptable to its own revelation. And in the Middle Ages they thought of the great classical pagan figures as *priori theologi*, the earliest theologians.

The danger of a tight and threatened Church, a Church that feels it must, at all costs, 'guard the deposit', is that the unspoken message it purveys is one of disbelief – you get the feeling that it is a man-made institution, which has to be protected with all the ingenuity of man. But wasn't the Pharisee Gamaliel wiser than that, when he said of the early Church, 'If this idea of theirs or its execution is of human origin, it will collapse; but if it is from God, you will never be able to put them down, and you risk finding yourselves at war with God.' (Acts 5: 38)?

Moreover, shouldn't this sense of freedom extend to the theological structures of the Church? Of course we need to hold on to and respect the insights of the past, but did the Holy Spirit really stop talking to man in about AD 150? If the Church clings desperately to all its precise definitions, isn't this another form of disbelief? Would God suddenly vanish if we felt we couldn't describe him in minutest detail? And is it so supremely important to be certain about the nature of Jesus now, when, if we believe in God, presumably we shall all be face-to-face at some time?

Freedom must extend to doubt and disbelief. If the Church is purely a man-made structure, then there can be no room for doubters, questioners or those who deny its truths; after all, if you get enough negative reactions they could pull

the whole structure down. But if we trust God, then we trust
that he can work through doubt, denial and disbelief; more
than that, if a Church is made up of people with adult
perceptions, then they will be well aware of the ambiguity of
life, the conflict of meaning and meaninglessness. Instead of
closing their eyes to the ambiguity, they live through it, and
so their faith is bound to be mixed with doubt, uncertainty
and a measure of disbelief – if there were no doubt in their
faith, it wouldn't be faith at all, but an ostrich-like burying of
their heads in the sand. 'There lives more faith in honest
doubt,' said Tennyson, 'believe me, than in half the creeds.'
Lessing said, 'A man who does not lose his reason over
certain things has none to lose.' Surely the same applies to
faith; if there were no possible event in the entire world that
could make me lose my faith, then I'm not sure that it would
be faith at all, but rather an illogical rigidity, even an
obsession. If you have such an obsession, then you are
obviously going to be deeply hostile to or fearful of anything
that seems to contradict it, and 'good' people are going to be
the ones you can get to agree with you.

I work in an area of London where about twenty thousand
people live, thousands commute in to work, and thousands
more tourists come to stay at the two hundred or so hotels.
*On Sundays, about two hundred and fifty people come to
church. Is everyone else wrong?* Have they nothing to say to
us? Must we assume that they have no interest in the
meaning of their lives or that they haven't fought and
suffered to reach some kind of understanding about their
existence? The more I talk to people outside the Church, the
more I find that they see it as something irrelevant and alien,
only to resort to at times of crisis if there's no one better to
hand, or for births, deaths and marriages, or as a place to
give up the struggle for meaning when the going gets too
tough; but really bearing no relation whatsoever to their
everyday lives or to anything that really matters to them.
This used to worry me, and I used to spend a lot of time and
energy thinking up ways to sell them the Miracle Elixir, but I
find that what I want to do now is simply to be with them, to
listen to their story and to learn from them – to pay attention

to them. And funnily enough, it's when I'm making the least demands on them, simply trying to love them and to be their servant, that they start taking what I believe in seriously and want to know about the things that have started me on my journey.

I said that we would try to look at the aspect of the Church that carries on the mission of Christ, but because it's so hidden and quiet I can't draw up a groundplan of it – I can only point in a rather impressionistic way to the places where I've found it, and perhaps try to generalise from there.

The real body of Christ starts from another form of 'God for nothing'. Thomas à Kempis wrote, 'O how powerful is the pure love of Jesus, which is mixed with no self-interest or self-love! Are not all those to be called mercenary who are ever seeking consolations? Do they not show themselves to be rather lovers of themselves than of Christ, who are always thinking of their own profit and advantage? *Where shall one be found who is willing to serve God for nothing?*' Amongst all the toys in the nursery, there was only one that had become real, only one Skin Horse. Really to follow Christ, to serve God for nothing, seems to me such a desperately hard road that it's no surprise that the true Church has been, and always will be, made up of only a few people. Nothing is new; in the fourteenth century Langland wrote his bitter attack on the Church in *Piers Plowman*, using Piers as the ideal of the spiritual life. The book doesn't have a happy ending, as the whole Church stagnates in a stupor, but there is a note of hope and defiance at the end: ' "Then by Christ," Conscience cried out, "I will become a pilgrim, and walk to the very ends of the earth in my search for Piers Plowman . . ." ' The image of the journey, the pilgrimage, the quest, are central to the Christian life.

When my brother was in his teens he became a Benedict-ine monk. The first thing that met you, as you entered his monastery, was a life-size statue of Jesus, holding out a crown of thorns with which to crown you. It's a very good image for the life they lead there, dedicated to the desper-ately tough school of prayer, serving God for nothing. It's also a painfully truthful reminder of what is involved for anyone who dares to serve God for nothing. In the parish

where I work now there is a small group of Franciscan friars
and, up the road, of Franciscan sisters, who follow the same
hard path. Their life of service and humility points to a
Christian truth which the Church as a whole must recover if
it deserves to survive.

Humility is not a highly regarded virtue nowadays; it can
have strong overtones of hypocrisy and false modesty, and
can be just another way of manipulating people by presenting a seemingly unaggressive front, like Uriah Heep, the
devious villain in *David Copperfield*. But true humility is
something that starts from strength. We are all so conditioned by a consumer society based on advertising and
marketing, that we feel we have to market ourselves and
package the product as successfully as possible. We need to
know that we are acceptable, popular, useful, powerful. But
true humility avoids both the trap of valuing oneself purely
as one is valued by others, and that of denying one's own
value and becoming an abject groveller. It takes as its
starting-point the religious sense of trust in Being and
self-acceptance. It is not easy to accept yourself; our pride
longs to deny, ignore or jettison all the dark and difficult
parts of our personalities, and it is a dangerous form of
self-love that makes us say, 'I must be perfect', making of
the religious life a self-improvement course. Just as humility
is grounded in paradoxical self-acceptance, so this humorous
acceptance and compassion should then flow out to everyone you meet: reverence, love and service for the other,
taking other people seriously as they are, where they are.

It is really only from a position of humility that you can
start to take other people seriously, in their own right,
without making any hidden claims on them. We live in a
society that is terrified of failure and solitude and anything
that can't be neatly labelled and categorised; and yet these
are three essential elements in the Christian journey: they
are the good earth in which humility is based. (The word
'humble' comes from the Latin word for earth, *humus*,
something that can be dry as dust and lifeless, or that can be
the rich ground of life. We have spoken before, when talking
about the cross, of the need to be firmly grounded in oneself
in order to be able to sustain the weight of the cross's open
arms.)

Humility starts with living one's life in the light of the cross, before God, trying to fulfil the tasks and answer the questions that life and God pose one as a unique individual. That is why the statue of Christ crowning you with a crown of thorns as you start your journey into the monastery is so truthful and strong. It means that in the end the only people one has to answer to are Christ and oneself – otherwise we fall into the trap of living other people's lives for them, of conforming and adapting to what is expected of us. Schopenhauer wrote: 'The sphere of what we are for other people is their consciousness, not ours; it is the kind of figure we make in their eyes, together with the thoughts which this arouses . . . people in the highest position in life, with all their brilliance, pomp, display, magnificence and general show, may well say: Our happiness lies entirely outside us, it exists only in the heads of others.'

Recently a group of Christian women were tortured in a Russian concentration camp in Siberia. They were made to stand barefoot on a frozen pond because they refused to stop singing the Easter Liturgy. Folly? Perhaps, but by staying true to their own journey and not conforming to the pressures of the system, they were doing so much that humility seeks to do: affirming the unique worth of the individual, confronting the guards with the responsibility for their own actions and perhaps challenging them to take stock of their own lives and values, and pointing to the 'and more' in life, the mystic element in our existence which resolutely refuses to be labelled or categorised. By almost any standard these women were failures; you can hardly be more useless or forgotten than is an inmate in a concentration camp, and yet simply by their being, by their staying true to themselves, they called into question a great empire and affirmed the values of the human spirit. A few defeated women were the Church, God's power coming to its full strength in weakness.

And what of solitude? Working in London you are constantly confronted with the desperate loneliness of so many people. And we struggle so hard to cover it up, all the way from constant background music to feverish over-working and to the mind-boggling pursuit of pleasure. But

humility, the Christian journey, really needs to start with the
awareness of aloneness before God. This is not the same as
'the flight of the alone to the Alone', which can be an escape
from the pain of becoming real and an avoidance of one's
responsibility for others, but has to do with the fact that
mankind desperately needs people who are not afraid to
confront their own aloneness – in Christian/Jewish terms, to
go out into the desert. It is a strange paradox that it is only
by withdrawing from people and the world that you are
given the strength to love them. Of course, there is always
the risk of the selfish withdrawal, running away from life and
burying one's head in the desert sand, but the true desert
experience is more *reculer pour mieux sauter* – standing back
in order to be able to jump further. The Christian desert
fathers lived in the wilderness in order to find out who they
really were, and people would come to them to learn from
the quality and austerity of their being about the challenge
and promise of existence.

In a world full of ambiguity and loneliness, this is what the
Church should be doing: humbly learning about itself and
waiting on God; a Church of people not afraid of their own
wounds, waiting on God in trust, and confronting all that is
so dehumanising in our culture.

But where are the churches that say to people, 'Don't be
afraid to be yourself'? All too often we have failed to
confront our own needs and pain, and when people come to
church looking for a resource against pain we go along with
them and try to find ways to ease it or make it less obvious;
we can't bear pain in them, because we can't bear it in
ourselves. But that is not where healing lies. Remember the
comment from Arthur Miller's *The Death of a Salesman*:
'Attention, attention must be finally paid to such a person.'

Attention doesn't mean rushing around or trying to
impose your own solutions or telling people to go on
holiday, join a prayer group, pull themselves together, trust
God, take up a hobby; attention means waiting with someone, being with them, accompanying them. Only they can
follow the path set before them – no one else can do it for
them – but to know that there is someone there who takes
them utterly seriously, who is within call, and who has

perhaps done their share of wrestling through the night – all
this gives courage to go on and to grow. The astonishing
thing about so many letters to the problem page was that
people would write back thanking you for advice, helpful
contacts and so on. But most of all they would just want to
say thank you for taking them seriously and for letting them
know that they mattered, that they were important. So often
there was no answer to give to a problem, but the fact that
someone had listened, had paid attention to them, without
trying to lessen the pain or draw a veil over it, seemed to
give them strength to go on, more confident to be themselves.

Humility comes into this too. When people come to
church in need, there must always be a part of them that
wants an answer, something clearly defined and reassuring,
and an equivalent response in us that wants to be useful and
to prove our worth. How easy it is for us to become social
workers. When my cat died when I was little, I insisted on
my parents telling me that he had gone to heaven. The
Church can go along with this, and if the clergy feel uneasy
they are only too happy to do so; perhaps they even do it out
of genuine kindness, because it seems to make the person
feel better. But such comfort is short-lived. By protecting
the person from her pain, we, the clergy, may be keeping
her childish, forcing her into a dependent attitude (and
where is the humility in that?), or we may be leaving her to
confront the worst alone. I've noticed so often with bereaved people, how very gentle they can be with other
people's feelings; they will smile and say, 'Thank you, that
makes me feel a lot better', and so we leave them alone and
go off thinking that we've done a good job of mopping up.

Perhaps humility recognises that there is nothing you can
do for a bereaved person; you are useless and empty. But
you an *be* with her, wait with her, pay attention to her, as she
confronts the night and the storm. The role of the servant is
to wait on her, not to tell her what to do. 'Welcome. Rest
here. Here is space and silence.' But how painful it is to
remain silent when we long to rush in with advice and
answers. Humbly to wait on someone, to pay attention to
her, often means silence and a sort of withdrawal – you

intrude as little of yourself as you can in order to leave as
much space as possible for her to explore her feelings. You
have no answers; only she has the answer and, if she is given
enough space and attention, then she may be able to hear
the call to her journey that is sounding through her pain.
Really to listen is so costly; it makes us feel helpless and
passive, the ear being the feminine part of the body, the
opening through which people come to us. If we talk enough
then our ears will be closed to them.

And there is another point of contact – our own wounds,
the places where our protective skin of self-assurance has
been pierced. Perhaps because we have been wounded
ourselves, we are able to meet others more directly. To
freeze and join the living dead, to try to retreat or run away,
to adopt unrealistic temporary escape routes – these are all
ways in which we react to crisis. But to have the courage to
seek one's own creative solution – then the suffering is not
all in vain and perhaps new life lies ahead. It is costly for the
listener and costly for the one who is listened to – God
knows how costly, but God is in the space, and the wound,
and God is in the voice that calls through the wound. And
God can cope with failure.

'Why? Why did God let my daughter die?' the mother
asked me, almost shaking me in her frantic desire for an
answer. What could I say? That life is a vale of soul-making
and it would help her to grow as a person? That I believed,
because of my faith in a suffering God, that her daughter
was safe? All I could say, blinking back my own tears and
feeling totally inadequate and useless, was, 'I don't know. I
don't know the answer.' Silence. The mother suddenly
relaxed and almost smiled. 'No,' she said, 'I don't think
there is one.' Everything in me cried out to make things
better for her, but in my very failure to do so I believe now
that the healing began: her own healing, in her own time, as
she set out on her lonely journey.

George Eliot wrote of 'the hardness of easy consolation'.
She also described the costly journey of waiting on someone,
and the effect it can have. 'He took one of her hands, and
clasped it as if they were going to walk together like two
children: it was the only way in which he could answer, "I

will not forsake you.'' And all the while he felt as if he were
putting his name to a blank paper which might be filled up
terribly.' In a sense, the paper *is* filled up terribly, at great
cost to both – Eliot speaks of 'thorn-pressure' – and yet in
the end 'it is better – it shall be better with me because I have
known you.' A suffering God is most strongly at work in
defeat.

And what of failure? Obviously only a masochist Church
would want to be a failure, but it is quite another thing not to
be afraid or ashamed to fail. I don't apologise for success,
but I worry if we see success in worldly terms. The Old
Testament, as Martin Buber pointed out, sees no intrinsic
value in success. If it has to report a successful deed it makes
certain that it also reports in detail all the failure involved in
the success. For the prophets, failure 'is the breath in their
nostrils' – they fight, but can never win.

> O Lord, thou hast deceived me, and I was deceived; thou
> art stronger than I, and thou hast prevailed. I have
> become a laughingstock all the day; everyone mocks me.
> For whenever I speak, I cry out, I shout, 'Violence and
> destruction!' For the word of the Lord has become for me
> a reproach and derision all day long. If I say, 'I will not
> mention him, or speak any more in his name', there is in
> my heart as it were a burning fire shut up in my bones, and
> I am weary with holding it in, and I cannot. [Jeremiah 20:
> 7-9]

Humility brings us back constantly to the figure of the
crucified, to the strange fact that the sense of the presence of
Being is often most vivid in the wretched and the broken.
When man is pared down to the bare bone by suffering, the
holy Being within him seems to participate in the agony, and
yet at the deepest level it is also the source of strength and
healing. Suffering, loss, pain, hurt, can strip away the
non-essentials, revealing the essence of a person. That
doesn't excuse suffering or make it something to pursue
deliberately, but it can mean that the place of suffering is
also a holy place. And we hate that, of course, and long to
gloss over it. 'Crucifixion? oh yes, too ghastly, but fortunate-
ly that unpleasant little incident is all in the past. Trium-

phant in his glory now . . .' And we act as if Calvary were all
a big mistake or, worse, as if God was only pretending; yes,
Jesus suffered, but it's all over now and he's very powerful
and triumphant, like a romantic novel where the poor
page-boy turns out to have been the heir to the throne all the
time. But unless the whole affair was a ghastly charade, a
sort of divine public relations exercise, then the humility,
powerlessness and self-giving love of Jesus was *the* expression of the meaning and purpose of our existence. Suffering
and failure we can be certain of; resurrection is a mystery
that we won't understand or experience until we've let
ourselves be crucified. The more we bandy it about as an
all-purpose salve or as the company logo, the more meaningless it becomes. First comes the cross. Could the Church
perhaps stop trying to prove its worth or to attract attention
or to be more successful, and just get on with the job of
loving people and, as Orwell suggested, getting broken up in
the process?

Humility, the desert, waiting, the folly of the cross. When
the Church really works, it's because it points to a reality
beyond itself. I'm not certain that the Church, based in
humility, can be too sure about exactly what that reality is,
but it should be saying, 'Look – open your eyes – see for
yourself.' There is nothing more deadening than to be told
that you must see or believe in a specific way. Of course, it
appeals to our desire for certainty and conformity to be told
'that's how it is', but the servant Church should be asking,
'And you, what do you say?' And somewhere there's a
fundamental lack of trust in God, in Being, if we believe that
without the Church's guidance people are going to go off the
rails. If you go to a serious play or movie you can find many
people who are following the quest for meaning as expressed
in dramatic terms and who are perhaps more open and alive
to the challenge of life in themselves and their fellow man
than the people who need to be fed a fixed-formula Miracle
Elixir. When the Church is humble towards such people,
listening rather than telling, then they in their turn are at
least prepared to take seriously the journey that the Church
believes in. Mankind come-of-age rightly rejects authority

figures, but it recognises the authority of sincerity and truth.
The Church tends to recognise the authority of learning and
of the pastoral office, but the real authority that anyone can
recognise tends to lie outside organised structures – the
authority of holiness, of authenticity.

Any two-bit teach-yourself guide to psychology will tell
you that the only possible starting-point for a healing
relationship or therapeutic alliance between counsellor or
analyst, and patient, is complete, non-judgemental acceptance. Only then can healing start; only then can the person
find the courage to face up to himself. That, surely, is the
love of God that the Church should be incarnating; the
humble love of the servant, God the mother. Ah but how
will people ever grow if they are always given unconditional
acceptance? There might indeed be a problem if we had all
our lives experienced nothing but love and acceptance, but
how many of us have? Usually it's the other way round; we
reach adult life convinced that we have to prove ourselves or
that life is hostile or indifferent to us. To meet acceptance
then may slowly, painfully, help us to slow down and stop
playing parts or manipulating people. Even if we have
experienced only acceptance, the pressure of life with its
endless questions and trials will prompt us into moving on.
The Church should be there to help that movement, not
trying to conceal the questions or provide pat answers.

True unconditional acceptance doesn't turn you into a
smug mummy's boy; it challenges you by making you aware
of your possibilities – all that you may become. There are
two groups of people to whom this doesn't quite apply: the
very rich, and the very poor. If your life is a constant
struggle against the pressure of poverty or oppression then
you have to be an exceptional person not to be simply worn
down by the pressure, unable to grow or respond but
becoming more and more like a beast of burden, trying to
shoulder your load. The Church should accept you there, of
course, but it should not accept the system that is doing this
to you. And maybe in fighting for you it will make mistakes,
but how can the Church, the body of Christ, remain silent
against the pressures that dehumanise man? For the very
rich it's more difficult. Accept them, love them, of course,

but they too are in danger of being dehumanised by the luxury that shields them from the pressures of life. Again, you need to be an exceptional person not to become more and more like an animal – not a beast of burden this time, but a fat Persian cat or, possibly, a vulture. How does the Church relate to such a person?

And surely a Church based on loving acceptance wants to help people to think for themselves, really to look and to make up their own minds. Wouldn't it be a Christian success story if someone came to church regularly and then decided, on mature reflection, that they couldn't accept the Christian viewpoint? Shouldn't we be glad that they care enough to wrestle with the problems and then to come to a decision which they feel makes sense for them? Better, surely, an empty church and a body of people who have left it, caring, compassionate, open to life and to others, than a church full of people meekly obeying orders and dutifully taking their elixir. Better still, I suppose, a church which can find room for all earnest inquirers after truth, without trying to force them into a mould.

We're back to belief. If we *really* believe, then we can expect to find the holy everywhere, in every corner of human life. It is only idols that can be kept locked up in a church, idols that we should be glad to escape from into the light of day. In James Joyce's *Portrait of the Artist as a Young Man*, the hero Stephen Dedalus has the overwhelming experience of suddenly realising that he is free from the deadly clutch of religion.

His throat ached with a desire to cry aloud, the cry of a hawk or eagle on high, to cry piercingly of his deliverance to the winds. This was the call of life to his soul not the dull gross voice of the world of duties and despair, not the inhuman voice that had called him to the pale service of the altar . . . What were they now but cerements shaken from the body of death – the fear he had walked in night and day, the incertitude that had ringed him round, the shame that had abased him within and without – cerements, the linens of the grave? His soul had arisen from the grave of boyhood, spurning her grave-clothes. Yes!

Yes! Yes! He would create proudly out of the freedom
and power of his soul, as the great artificer whose name he
bore, a living thing, new and soaring and beautiful,
impalpable, imperishable.

And yet why should religion be deadly? 'The call of life to
his soul' is the *start* of the religious journey. The call of
Being says, '*Be*', be yourself, do not try to be a saint,
fainting at the sight of anything human, but get on with life,
loving people, accepting them, making mistakes, getting
dirty, fighting against all the pressures of the night to be on
the side of healing. And when someone really has the
courage to be himself, accepting the ambiguity of light and
shadow both in himself and in creation, then he brings
healing to others. Of all the Christians who have really
helped me, I think of those who didn't claim to have all the
answers, who didn't make a great song and dance about
being a Christian or being saved or any of that rubbish (if the
Ark had sailed, they would probably have been left behind
looking after the flood victims), and who had to grapple with
a strong feeling of not wanting to be Christian, powerful
feelings of doubt, anger, boredom, fed-upness, grief, pain
and despair. Above all, they were *human*: real, three-
dimensional human beings that you could laugh and cry
with. If you meet someone who has that depth of acceptance
of life, of himself and of you, then you begin to have the
courage to be real yourself, to start on your journey, and to
take up arms in the cause of life.

And because the struggle is all around us, there are battles
to be fought – little, puny everyday battles – if we have the
grace and courage to try and incarnate God's suffering love
in the world.

. . . the fervour of sympathy with which we contemplate a
grandiose martyrdom is *feeble* compared with the enthu-
siasm which keeps unslacked where there is no danger, no
challenge – nothing but impartial mid-day falling on
commonplace, perhaps half-repulsive, objects which are
really the beloved ideas made flesh. Here undoubtedly
lies the chief poetic energy: – in the force of imagination
that *pierces or exalts the solid fact, instead of floating*

among cloud-pictures. To glory in a prophetic vision of
knowledge covering the earth, is an easier exercise of
believing imagination than to see its beginning in newspaper placards, staring at you from a bridge beyond the
cornfields; and it might well happen to most of us dainty
people that we were in the thick of the battle of
Armageddon without being aware of anything more than
the annoyance of a little explosive smoke and struggling
on the ground immediately about us. [George Eliot; *my
italics*]

The holy is there, in the market-place, the launderette, in
Sainsbury's; wherever people live, or suffer, or are concerned with finding the most creative human values, Being is
at work, just as Christ met people in the centre of their lives,
not in the uninhabited religious outlands. Ideally, Church
ritual, which can seem so camp, lifeless or irrelevant, should
be the guardian of this vision. In the stillness and mystery,
we begin to sense the presence of the holy which underlies
the simplest everyday things and people. That's why the
Church shouldn't be an escape or an irrelevance, a place
where you put on a false front, but the place where you are
given time and space to sense the deepest levels of your
existence, the reality underlying all things.

If people are turned off by the Church, is it partly because
we have become so verbal and precise in our liturgies that
we have left no room for mystery? People may knock the old
Latin mass of my childhood, and of course, there's a lot to
be said for using a language you can understand, but at least
we were taught a different and important sort of prayer
above and beyond words; a stillness and silence and a
waiting on God. Now you have to wade your way through at
least fourteen paragraphs, sub-paragraphs and codicils about the nature and activity of God, which may bring
intellectual assent but, in the end, so what?

Ursula le Guin wrote of 'a space, a time like this, between
act and act, when you may stop and simply be. Or wonder
who, after all, you are.' Isn't one of the greatest gifts of the
Church the chance to offer such a space? And isn't it in
danger of snatching it back if it shows itself frightened of

mystery, solitude, failure, darkness – of everything, in fact, that confronts us most with the pressure of Being? 'Not by might, nor by power, but by my Spirit, says the Lord of hosts' (Zechariah 4:6). Simple, ordinary everyday things, broken, humble and powerless; bread, wine and water, the Skin Horse, a man in a pub, women tortured with hypothermia and ice-burns; everything, including life itself, becomes a sacrament, the humble place where the mystery breaks through. The Church, the body of Christ, rips the grave-clothes from us and says, 'Get up. Walk. Look. See. Rejoice.' And for every hundred churches carefully wrapping people up in a cocoon of comfort and death, suffocating them with might and power and authority and man-made institutions, the spirit of truth will surely break through in at least one, and say, 'You are a living thing, new and soaring and beautiful, impalpable, imperishable; take up your bed, and walk.'

One final word about the true body of Christ – and I make no apology if I find one of its most potent descriptions in the work of a man who described himself as 'a democrat who loves mankind and denies the gods' and whom someone else described as a man who 'did not affect certainty where he found mystery'. Shelley gets a bad press nowadays for wishy-washy images and sentiments, perhaps for running the same sort of risk that I run in writing a book like this – 'Fine words butter no parsnips', as my old aunt used to say. In other words, so what? What's it got to do with me and reality? But Shelley's idealism, like Plato's on which it was based, is not an unrealistic dream but rather founded on a sober awareness of the savage realities of life. Plato and Shelley knew that the ideal state, person, life cannot be brought about, but that the ideal coexists in constant contrast and dialectic with life; ideal and real are held in tension. Shelley tries to show what men have made of life, contrasted with what they might make of it. Would it be too much to call him a missionary? 'Until the mind can love, and admire, and trust, and hope and endure, reasoned principles of moral conduct are seeds cast upon the highway of life which the unconscious passenger tramples into the dust, although they would bear the harvest of his happiness.'

In Shelley's *Prometheus Unbound* there is a god of
triumph and self-glorification, Jupiter, who keeps mankind
enslaved with 'knee-worship, prayer and praise', 'with fear
and self-contempt and barren hope'. (Come back Freud and
Feuerbach, all is forgiven . . .) Prometheus is chained to a
rock, tortured by visions of the suffering of mankind, but at
the moment of his greatest suffering, failure and despair, he
is released because of his unquenched mercifulness and trust
in love. Jupiter is cast down from his throne, to be impris-
oned in the abyss, although the threat of his return is always
there; but for mankind to live in hope, freed from the pale
service at the altar of the god 'out there', love is the way
forward:

> Love, from its awful throne of patient power
> In the wise heart, from the last giddy hour
> Of dread endurance, from the slippery, steep,
> And narrow verge of crag-like agony, springs
> And folds over the world its healing wings.
>
> Gentleness, Virtue, Wisdom, and Endurance,
> These are the seals of that most firm assurance
> Which bars the pit over Destruction's strength;
> And if, with infirm hand, Eternity,
> Mother of many acts and hours, should free
> The serpent [Jupiter] that would clasp her with his length;
> These are the spells by which to reassume
> An empire o'er the disentangled doom.

In other words, if the true Church gets swallowed up by
mechanical toys and Miracle Elixir, or simply loses heart
when confronted by all the pressures of the night and of
meaninglessness, this is the way forward.

> To suffer woes which Hope thinks infinite;
> To forgive wrongs darker than death or night;
> To defy Power, which seems omnipotent;
> To love, and bear; to hope till Hope creates
> From its own wreck the thing it contemplates;
> Neither to change, nor falter, nor repent;
> This, like thy glory, Titan, is to be
> Good, great and joyous, beautiful and free;

This is alone Life, Joy, Empire, and Victory.

I know that there's a danger with such grand, unexamined concepts flying around that our minds, conditioned by Wardour Street and Hollywood's sobbing violins, will relapse into a comfy coma. 'How beautiful; how noble,' we contentedly sigh, pouring another glass of Lotus liqueur. And a 'religious' book has so many lovely words and stories to offer the reader – God, resurrection, peace, joy, love – all in danger of being equally meaningless, so that the reader risks being battered to death with cotton wool and plummy sentiments. Fine words butter no parsnips. But Prometheus was chained to the rock for three thousand years before he found freedom. I suppose that those verses of Shelley are in danger of sounding empty unless taken in the context of all the agony that has gone before – and may come again. And if I talk loudly and contentedly about God and the Church, then that will be empty, too.

I've brought a motley crowd of witnesses with me for this chapter – a Titan chained to a rock, tortured women, a desolate man in a pub – but I hope that they are enough to puncture the rhetoric, to say something about the Church, the body of Christ. A man, crowned with thorns, holds out a crown of thorns. Where is the glory? In a God who suffers, good for nothing regal or splendid, but there in failure and brokenness and pain; and in the people who endure 'thorn-pressure', serving God for nothing. No easy answers, now or ever. The Church gets on with shouldering the cross, carrying the whole weight of the conflict between meaning and meaninglessness; waiting on man, and waiting on God.

> God doth not need
> Either man's work or his own gifts. Who best
> Bear his mild yoke, they serve him best, his State
> Is Kingly. Thousands at his bidding speed
> And post o'er Land and Ocean without rest:
> They also serve who only stand and wait.
>
> (Milton, *On His Blindness*)

7 The essential paradox

It's all very well to keep pointing out problems, but not so easy to try to find solutions. This chapter is an attempt to give a few answers, or point in the direction where I believe answers are to be found, though I fear that I'm going to end up following Shelley, hovering unhappily between the ideal and the real.

First of all, the Church. How do we bridge the gap between the Church of chapter 5 and the Church of chapter 6? Perhaps we can't. Perhaps the important thing is to have a constant dialectic between the two. And perhaps just as we need to have a sense of humour about ourselves, so we need to have a sense of humour about the Church. I often don't know whether to laugh or cry, but if we believe, as Julian of Norwich believed – 'I thought it quite impossible that everything should turn out well . . . but "what is impossible to you is not impossible to me. I shall honour my word in every respect, and I will make everything turn out well" – then perhaps the Church is a comedy rather than a tragedy. It is a means to an end, here for only one reason, to convey the presence of Christ, and when it starts giving itself airs or getting pompous and lordly, then maybe a good raspberry will bring it to its senses. Servants don't sit on thrones.

So many of the problems of the Church have to do with the fear of freedom. As we have seen, because freedom causes anxiety, people use the Church as an escape from personal freedom. Obviously, if you join an organisation, you want it to be strong and capable, and you want its officer class to be powerful figures that you can respect and take orders from. There is a double loss of freedom, a pact between warder and prisoner, as you hand over responsibility to the warder and he loses his own freedom by allowing (or wanting?) you to do so. But at the risk of repetition, I must emphasise that the idea of the servant is not just empty rhetoric. Clergy, bishops, archdeacons, deans, vicars, curates, cardinals, popes, ministers really are very *unimportant*; if necessary, we should dump the lot, because the only absolute imperative for the Church is that it must fulfil its mission. If we could only get that into our thick skulls, the freedom it would give us would be amazing. But, of course, freedom is just as threatening to an organisation as to an individual, because it implies growth and change.

Freedom is always limited by the circumstances in which we find ourselves, and the Church is almost snowed under with the weight of its heritage. For a start, there's the sheer physical reality of thousands of ancient buildings, full of ancient treasures, all needing money, time and energy for their upkeep. Perhaps even more burdensome is the weight of people's expectations. The Church is supposed to be the guardian of moral truths, a focus for religious feeling, a social club, a theatre, social services, a museum, a chaplaincy for people too hurt by life to dare go out there again. And its functionaries – well, knowing the pressure of the expectations that are thrust on to me as a mere curate, I can imagine what it must be like if you are in a more responsible position. No wonder people get frozen into their expected roles.

But in the end, we either succumb to other people's fantasies of our role, or we accept the challenge and pain of being real. You can't suddenly institutionalise the desire to be real, or send out announcements from Canterbury and Rome that from Monday we're all going to try to be Skin Horses, but you can make a stand as an individual and perhaps give others the courage to do the same. And if we dare to accept that the Church can be free and flexible, then we can have a sense of humour and a sense of detachment about its institutions. I once talked to a very eminent Jesuit professor, who said that we all tend to think of the Church as being terribly frail and doddery, like an old maiden aunt on her last legs, when in fact the Church may well just be in its infancy, still trying to learn to walk. If we *really* trust God, Being, meaning, and we believe that the Church is *only* here to live out the continuing presence and ministry of Christ, not its own, then surely we can have the courage to be free and to stop pandering to people's expectations, and above all to stop pretending to be grand when we are called to be servants. The Church which worships God can afford to be free, because it trusts God. The Church which worships a comfort blanket (or itself) can't afford to relax for a moment, because the magic might fade, and it needs impressive man-made structures and functionaries to keep the show on the road: a plurality of father figures to keep us obedient and safe at night.

If the Christian – or non-Christian – can keep at the forefront of his mind the image of the crucified, of the foot-washer and the servant, of the man whose kingly array was not priceless silk and gold but a crown of vicious thorns (and if you've seen those Middle Eastern thorns you'll know that they are not the little prickles we get in Britain), then he can afford a humorous, affectionate detachment from all in the Church that runs so counter to the gospel. He can afford, like the boy in Hans Andersen's story, to say, 'Look, the emperor's got no clothes on.' When the emperor/Church stops trying to rule and direct people, and realises that

> Those he commands move only in command,
> Nothing in love; now does he feel his title
> Hang loose upon him, like a giant's robe
> Upon a dwarfish thief [*Macbeth*, Act V, Scene 2]

then perhaps it will be free to repent, to go out into the desert, to rediscover awe and mystery and wonder, above all to rediscover its role of humble service.

What freedom from servitude if the Church could say, 'I am not the emperor; my imperial clothing is a farce; my place is to follow a man who was born in a stable, became a refugee, was tried by the desert experience, asked nothing of people but to take themselves seriously, and was murdered by the authorities. What "authority" I have is different from any other: it is the authority of trying to be real, of serving and of suffering'; the authority of not wanting to be 'saints' if that means not being human, refusing to bow down to all the pressures of the night, and striving to the utmost and in every circumstance to be on the side of life – to be healers. If you, the Church, can strip yourself of the weight of other

people's expectations and of traditions which no longer help
to convey the presence of Christ as they once did, then you
will be stripped for action, ready to look critically at yourself
and decide how best to fulfil the Christian essentials in the
present circumstances – and if that means a five-person
papacy made up of Chinese women, then *why not*? There
will be mistakes and failures, of course, but if Christ is the
head of the Church surely we can trust him, rather than
staying in a threatened little enclave, backs to the wall,
chaps, protecting a little old God and a little old Church.

And what of the little old doctrines? Being 'a professor of
the fact that another suffered' seems so irrelevant today.
We, the clergy, bat around all these strange terms like
'kingdom of God', 'resurrection', 'heavenly father' and so
on, without anyone really understanding or caring what
we're talking about; we see ourselves as having a paternal,
teaching role towards the world and then we can't understand why the world finds us as relevant as a Victorian box of
children's aspirins. And yet why did the Church happen in
the first place? Surely what converted people from Greek
paganism wasn't a book of rules and doctrines, but a totally
new experience of living? The early Churchmen weren't
professors but people who loved and served and who, above
all, knew that they were loved. It was the quality of their
living and the spirit of their community that converted men.
And shouldn't it be the same for us today? As servants,
Christians should be extremely diffident about offering
people doctrine; what we do have, and what we should bring
when we *collaborate* with the rest of mankind (servants work
with and *for* people – they don't try to take them over) is the
unique and agonising inspiration of the crucified man, and
our attempt to live our lives in and by his light.

And what about the Bible? The more threatened you feel,
or the more desperately you need to feel certain and to
reject ambiguity, the more you will need a totem or ultimate
authority figure. We have varieties of totems in the Church –
individual men or women like the Pope and other charismatic figures; the magic of the sacraments; devotion to revolu-
tionary theories or, on the other hand, middle-class morality
('If Jesus had seen *that* woman daring to show her face in

church,' said a woman at a local church, 'he'd have turned in
his grave'); the system itself; and, of course, the Bible. The
danger of all these is the same, and is evident if you examine
the logic of the woman's remark: *if* Jesus had
seen . . . he'd have turned in his *grave* – in other words, he
isn't here to see anything, and for all the good he does he
might as well be buried (and forgotten) except for pious
remarks and sentiments. His radical love and acceptance for
everyone can be safely buried away too. No challenge of new
life here.

Once you have got Jesus out of the way, though, you need
something or someone to fill his place: hence the totems,
and hence the potential idolatry of a book. I don't want to
offend people who call the Bible 'the word of God', but I'm
no longer very sure what that means. The idea of God using
humans as automatic dictating machines or of somehow
magically guiding them so as to reveal hidden truths without
error, may give doctrines and scriptures an impressive
weight of authority ('It's got to be right because God says so
in the Bible . . . '), but it rides most uneasily with any
thought of man's free response to God, the ambiguity of
existence, and the very nature of God himself. What would
it mean to say that Being-itself or the experience of ultimate
meaning in existence had 'dictated' or 'inspired' the scriptures? Surely it's much closer to all we've been trying to say,
to understand the scriptures as the attempt of many different
authors, working in different cultures, times and traditions;
to grasp their understanding of the *mysterium tremendum et
fascinans* (the *mystery*, not a who's who of heavenly bodies)
as it is revealed through particular people (like Jesus) and
events, traditions and folk-history passed down to them,
theological speculation, and the political movements of
ancient near-Eastern history.

To call the Bible the 'word of God' also seems a dangerous oversimplification of what we actually have in front of
us. It suggests certainty and infallibility when there is none
there, rather as if, when your father told you that every
cloud has a silver lining, you started aiming metal-detectors
at the sky, instead of realising that he was making a
statement about the way he sees life. We have already

looked briefly at how the gospel writers worked over and
arranged the material handed down to them about Jesus,
and how the authors of Matthew and Luke revised, cen-
sored, rearranged and unravelled in a creative, meditative
way what they thought were the religious implications of
Mark's terse and mysterious little book. Take, as another
example, the way the author of Chronicles feels free to
rewrite the history of Israel as given in the books of Kings
and Samuel, in order to make theological points for the time
in which he was writing; his concern was not to be a
historian, but to create a moral tale for his contemporaries.
Thus the dying David's last words are changed from a list of
enemies to be rubbed out, that would do credit to any Mafia
godfather, to a beautiful prayer incorporating all the
approved theological insights of the Chronicler's time.

The more you look at the Bible and all the studies that
have been done on it, the harder it is to understand it as
anything but the words of men. It is the work of scores of
anonymous writers, often using traditional material that had
been handed on to them. Even people who claim that the
whole Bible is God's inspired word, tend to apply a filtering
technique in practice. This bit is more God's word than that
bit – for instance, they may feel that passages in the psalms
about dashing babies' heads against a stone are less useful
than the ten commandments. But once you start saying that
one part is less inspired than another you are getting into a
difficult area, because the question then arises of how you
decide what is inspired or uninspired – what are your
criteria? And in the end we usually choose the bits we like or
that fit in with our cultural preoccupations and prejudices,
zeroing in on vital words of God to do with the eternal
damnation of homosexuals, or letting pass the bits that God
must have written on an off day about the vital religious
importance of women keeping their big mouths shut. If all
scripture *is* the word of God, how can you determine that
one part is more godly than another except by using your
human (fallible) intellect, or by claiming that God is guiding
you (and how do you decide that?)?

I wish there were space here to list all the different
theologies that the Bible contains (all the different

approaches to what 'the kingdom of God' might mean in the
New Testament, for example, or all the contrasting covenant
theologies in the Old Testament, or the conflict between the
way the prophets approached God and the other ways
advocated), just to show what a library of diversity it is, and
what a glorious tribute it is to the searching after truth of the
human spirit. To call it the 'word of God,' appeals to our
childish need for certainty while stifling our God-given gifts
of intellect and questioning. Isn't the way forward to say that
the Bible has no authority *in itself*; it is a human document
and thus liable to human error? Its words are not dictated by
God, but they are a witness to revelation, the attempt by
those many anonymous writers over many generations to
encapsulate their vision of the 'and more' in existence, the
revelation of God as they experienced it in particular people
or events or in contemplating their own lives. The Bible is
words about the Word of God, and its authority comes from
what it points to, not what it is in itself.

What I'm working towards, with both Bible and doctrine,
is a certain distancing from our Western obsession with
verbal formulae – the all-powerful written word. We tend to
think of God's will as revealed in forms of words, propositions, creeds, and so on – and obviously I must be careful not
to devalue words too much, since man is a linguistic being –
but I have an uneasy feeling that the moment you tie
something down in words, it may cease to be real. Somehow
the life goes out of it, like a tiger that one moment was alive
and free, and the next is gathering dust, stuffed and
mounted under a glass case. The man who wrote down and
thus recorded for posterity the Scottish and border ballads,
also destroyed them as a living art form, because after that
no one felt free to tinker with them or add to them (which
was roughly how they were created in the first place, by the
co-creativity of the group). Suddenly they were 'poetry' and
began to fossilise on the printed page, to be studied rather
than lived. Chesterton said that 'truths turn into dogmas the
moment they are disputed', and that's what happened to
Christian truth. Now we are left with a vast corpus of printed
material about which we are expected to think, but with
which we are also expected to agree. God's chief desire

seems to be to want us to believe in him, and to join the appropriate sect.

But pursuing the road of thought and logic in religion is ultimately self-defeating. We will end up as professors of paradox, because, contrary to all that Aristotelian logic would have us believe, ultimate reality is so far beyond our capacity to understand it that the closest we can come through thinking is to paradoxical logic: a secret that Eastern religion has long understood. Paradoxical logic says things like 'it is and it is not' or 'it is neither this nor that', maddening to our logical Western minds and yet, perhaps, closer to an adult perception of reality. Lao-tse wrote, 'The highest we can reach is to know and yet think we do not know; it is a disease not to know and yet to think we do know.' In the West, paradoxical logic underlies Marxist and Hegelian theories of dialectics, and Jung said that reality is so complex it can best be expressed by paradox. Comfort-blanket religion finds paradox anathema because it makes simple answers seem inadequate.

But isn't part of the way forward, for Christian and non-Christian alike, to stop ascribing to man-made books and definitions a power and authority beyond what they merit? 'A religion without mystery must be a religion without God,' said Jeremy Taylor, the great Anglican divine. Mystery and precise verbal definitions are uneasy bedfellows, and if we come to religion for security, then any hint of mystery is going to give us sleepless nights, but if we go back to the Bible in search of doctrine we'll find no elaborate formulae. Indeed in the Old Testament you repeatedly read that anyone who sees God will die. Jesus didn't demand intellectual assent to a set of propositions, and St Paul is at pains to point out that what knowledge we have is partial – the essential element is faith, which comes from God, not from speculation.

Some people today are embarrassed even to use the word 'God', or embarrassed when he/she/it is brought up in conversation, and perhaps this is a healthy sign because, far from signalling atheism or ignorance, it may well be that they know they are broaching areas of mystery where silence is wiser and more respectful than the endless babble of people who rabbit on about God as if he were a cookery recipe. 'It is no use walking anywhere to preach,' said St Francis, 'unless we preach as we walk.' Should the Church now accept that it will never be able to grasp ultimate reality by thought alone, but that the experience of unity behind the paradox comes only from living and acting the love of God? And perhaps the sort of teaching role the Church should adopt is not that of instilling knowledge into people, but the more important teaching that comes unspoken and unformalised, simply from being in the presence of a mature, loving person. You can programme a robot to say what you want it to say, but it is the example of your being, not your words, that inspires reverence for life, reverence for mystery, in another person.

People are frightened or sceptical about Christians because they sense that the words we utter and the creeds we follow are not as simple as we would like to make out, and perhaps that we would like to turn them into robots or smother them in our own comfort blankets. They neither understand nor care about half the words we toss around so lightly (words like God and eternal life, for example) because they seem to have no relevance to their lives and, perhaps more importantly, no relevance to *our* lives, except as part of the structure that any comfort-religion needs to keep up the safety barriers between the believers and reality. Feuerbach wrote that 'by his God thou knowest the man, and by the man his God'. The more certain and strident the call to faith and the vision of God, the less happy I am about the humanity of the Christian who makes that call (or devotee of any other religion, for that matter). It's the obsessive-compulsive patients in psychiatrists' waiting-rooms who have to have everything 'just so'; the frightened child in the nursery who needs to be certain what every noise is and to know that the night-light will never go out. To encounter a Christian with a real reverence for the mystery of existence and the mystery of another's being, as well as a reverence for himself, is to get a very vivid, if unspoken, idea of the heart of Christian belief. I would like to think that that could be the way forward for the Church, bashing its Bible a little less forcefully, drumming in its doctrines a little less demandingly. The ideal servant speaks seldom, if ever; he/she gets on with the job. Perhaps we need to walk a lot more, and preach a lot less.

Elenora Duse, the great actress, once burst out, 'To save the Theatre, the Theatre must be destroyed, the actors and actresses all die of the Plague . . . they make art impossible.' Well, I'm trying, a little desperately, to resolve a few problems in this chapter, and a *cri de coeur* like Duse's sounds so appealing. To save the Church, we need to kiss goodbye to all our professors of certainty, our academics, and *get on with the job.* Feuerbach called for us to cancel above all the old cleavage between this side and the beyond in order that humanity might concentrate on itself, its world and its present with all its heart and soul.' And as Alexander Pope wrote:

> Know then thyself, presume not God to scan,
> The proper study of mankind is man.

The obsession with an afterlife, assuring one's personal survival, and with glorifying some remote entity at the expense of devaluing humanity, seems almost sacrilegious. Surely what matters, for Christian and non-Christian alike, is how one chooses to live life *now*, and how one attempts to answer the terrible questions that confront humanity.

Kierkegaard's alternative to being a 'professor of the fact' was actually to suffer oneself. To follow Jesus in his radical approach to human relationships can certainly ensure that. Never to condemn your fellow man means that you lose all power or leverage over others. (But servants aren't here to judge.) To love your enemies is frightening; it means wanting the best for the people who can hurt you worst and it makes you totally vulnerable. (Yet the servant is always vulnerable to his masters.) To forgive and go on forgiving, to break the chain of evil by returning good for bad – it's hard to think of a better recipe for suffering, but what else can a servant do, except resign? A Church which tries to incarnate sacrificial love is bound to suffer, but that suffering brings healing for others. And when the Church really suffers with and for people, you sometimes get an inkling that suffering and evil are not the final realities. The resurrection points to something beyond, but unfortunately you can't be a professor of the fact that there was a resurrection – you can only confront the cross head-on and find your own way from there. To meet a Viktor Frankl or a Christian Skin Horse is to be given a sort of answer, and the courage to go on to find your own.

And as we have seen, suffering can be creative, can help you to be more truly yourself. I had a long correspondence with a woman who wrote to the problem page, initially because her husband and children had been killed in a motorway accident. She went through a series of nervous breakdowns, ending up in a mental hospital. One morning she woke up and walked through the hospital grounds down to the river nearby. She had a vague, unformed idea of throwing herself in. But as she walked, she suddenly had the strange feeling of being at home in her body again, of compassion, almost love, for herself – her hands, her arms, her legs, which had been through so much. She thought to herself, 'Life has thrown the worst it can at me; I have been to the bottom of the abyss but I am still here. The rest, whatever it may be, I can endure.' From that moment, healing began. Nothing would ever take away the agony she had endured, but it was as if she could slowly begin a new life, perhaps more fully herself than ever before.

In *The Wizard of Oz*, Dorothy, the tin man, the cowardly lion and the scarecrow all set off to find the Wizard, the godlike figure who will give them the solution to their problems and change them into what they want to be. When they finally reach the Wizard after many trials and tribulations, they discover that he's just an ordinary man with problems of his own. But they also discover that the very quest for him has effected the sought-after changes in them; they had the answer within themselves all the time. Suffering may be the pressure that calls us to be ourselves. That's not a justification for it and doesn't excuse it, but somehow that same destructive force can be the flame and the anvil which forges us.

I wish I could stop there, because any other attempt at an answer threatens to become academic and sterile. Let the enthroned, kingly God 'out there' come up with a book of

answers as to why we suffer. But the kingship of God was
demonstrated in 'behold your king, who comes to you in
gentleness', in service, sacrifice and suffering; very few
answers there – rather, a promise and a hope. The existence
of suffering, evil and death in the world is usually seen as
one of the great stumbling-blocks to belief. The classic
response to this centres on the idea of free will. If we lived in
a perfect world, without ambiguity, then belief in God
would be as easy as falling off a log and there wouldn't be
much point (or credit?) to it; life is a vale of soul-making,
and we are refined by suffering and learn and grow because
of it.

You can just about get away with an answer like that (and
it can be put far more persuasively by a skilled theologian) if
you apply it to aware adults who may be able to make some
sense of their suffering, but what about children? In the end,
you have to extend the time scale beyond death, and say that
the explanation or restitution will be given then. I'm not
going to waste your time or mine by proposing theories
about suffering and death being due to sin or the Garden of
Eden. The sort of vindictive, unpleasant God who doles out
punishment like that is not only unworthy of worship but
probably also, when he is not condemning people to eternal
damnation, spends his free time pulling the wings off flies
and cherubs. I think I can understand, though, that for man
to be free and capable of growth, he needs to be in an
environment that challenges him. They say that dolphins
have a brain capacity almost equal to man's, but have never
had to develop it because they are so perfectly adapted to
their environment. If we lived in a world where it was
impossible for us to hurt others or to suffer, wouldn't we
remain incredibly bland and childlike? There would never
be any reason to learn, grow or ask questions. It has been
one of the central threads of this book that it is in the
questions that life asks us that growth and meaning are to be
found. People who evade the questions, or who are
cocooned against them, threaten to lapse back into non-
being, to lose all the most precious parts that go to make
them human; if you don't believe me, try going to a jet-set
party or being a deb's delight for a season, or going to a

church that gives people all the answers. Perhaps death, the final question, works in the same way. How precious would life or time be to us if there were no end to them? I fear death, but I can't think of anything more deadly than just going on and on and on. Death is the context which makes life so precious.

There's a rather cruel story about a mediaeval king who gave his new court jester the fool's sceptre and told him to keep it until he met a bigger fool than himself. Some years later the king was dying and sent for the jester. 'I'm going on a long journey,' he said. 'Where are you going, and how long for?' asked the jester. 'I don't know,' replied the king. 'Have you made any provision for the journey?' 'No.' The jester handed the king his fool's sceptre: 'Then this belongs to you.'

The days of frightening people into religion by fear of death or damnation are, I hope, long gone. As we said earlier, belief based on hope of reward or escaping death has no moral value, but is more like opportunism or pragmatism, *sauve qui peut*. And yet it seems extraordinary that in a world where, as Benjamin Franklin wrote, 'nothing can be said to be certain, except death and taxes', we spend hours filling out forms or dreaming up tax dodges, and push to the back of our minds the fact that someday – tomorrow? 1995? – we will die, and although it is a brutal and unpalatable fact, it is the very awareness of it which gives such preciousness to time, people and events.

It was in the context of his approaching death that the condemned man, Meursault, in Camus' *The Outsider*, could look back on his life and realise that he was happy. Tolstoy's *Death of Ivan Ilyich* is about the almost parallel experience of an elderly man, who suddenly learns that he is about to die. His life has been meaningless, just wasted time, but his sudden awareness of this and of his approaching death forces him actually to confront his situation – to be aware of himself, where he is, and to face up to himself and his life. And by having the courage to do this, he rises above himself and finds meaning not only for the present but even for his past life. The past, what you are because of what you have been, is a possession that no one can take away from you;

you could almost say that 'having been' is the surest kind of being. That's why living in the present is so desperately important, actually experiencing your life to the full *now*, the pain, joy, hope, boredom, fear, rather than relapsing into unreal dreams of the future or living on nostalgia. Awareness of death as 'time's winged chariot hurrying near' gives a context and meaning to life – or rather, urges you to find one.

Those who have had the painful privilege of working with the dying, and in particular, perhaps, in the hospices for the dying, are often able to witness a transformation in someone who knows that he is dying, as he moves through the stages of rejection, anger, fear and depression to a sort of *plateau* of acceptance where he has come to terms with himself and his fate. It is a progression often closely mirrored by the tragic heroes, but this time it is real. The time just before death often becomes, for the dying person and his or her family, one of intense shared emotion – not necessarily all unhappy, by any means – as under the pressure of time they are able to express their deepest feelings and love. And often there is peace, and the end comes not as the terrifying obliteration we all dread, but with calm, even gentleness.

Much of our fear must be because we are dealing with the unknown:

The undiscovered country from whose bourn
No traveller returns . . .

and yet in a way, that's precisely the point: it *is* the unknown, and we don't know for certain that death is the ultimate reality. I'm reluctant to start talking about ghosts, because I don't know how much their existence might prove, nor that they can really mean much to us unless we have experienced them for ourselves. But what are interesting are the independently conducted studies of people like Moody, Kübler-Ross, Gallup and Sabom into near-death experiences, where people have been clinically dead and then brought back to life. What is astonishing is the uniformity of people's accounts. They were aware of their deaths, sometimes of looking down on their own bodies and sometimes of travelling through a dark tunnel towards a bright light, coupled with a strong sense of reality, an absence of pain, and feelings of tranquillity and even delight. It has been suggested that this may be caused by the body releasing beta-endorphine – a sort of natural opiate – but this doesn't really explain how people were able to record in detail things like monitor readings or conversations over their corpses which, clinically, they should have been able neither to see nor hear. You can't prove anything by such experiences, but that whole difficult realm of the paranormal is perhaps a warning to us not to take death too literally. Here, as so often, there is hope, of course, and fear, but no certain answer – nor do I think that the fact of death proves or disproves the question of God, Being, meaning. It poses the question of meaning in its starkest form.

It seems inappropriate to talk about 'blaming' God for death or suffering if you are working in the context of meaning versus meaninglessness, but for the sake of argument you can try to lessen the blame on God in various ways. In terms of world politics, the lack of a vision of God seems to bring more suffering than God himself. If politicians and states had the religious view of reverence and love for each single human life, how drastic a diminution in world suffering might there be? You might say that there is not too much but too little religion in the world today.

The religious vision of the sanctity of human life should also be applied to the suffering due to natural causes like famine and disease. Natural forces produce the initial disaster, but if man were wholehearted in his response, without regard to political or financial gain, the suffering could be greatly lessened. It is not God's fault that man spends more time, effort and money on devising weapons of destruction than on working to rid the world of hunger and illness. Nor is it God's fault that the roots of many of modern man's trials like cancer and heart disease seem to lie in mental and environmental pressures on the body. We are only just starting to learn how closely man's mind and body are linked – how he allows himself to become ill and, sometimes, how the power of his mind/heart/spirit/will can cure the medically 'incurable'.

So you can produce various arguments to lessen the blame

on God. But how do I explain any of that to the little boy down the road with all the drainage tubes coming out of his skull, where the medics have tried to remove the cancer in his brain? Do I tell his mother that she will be a better woman because of it? The danger of all the arguments that try to justify the ways of God to man is that you are liable to feel rather like a laboratory rat put through a series of tests and mazes to see how well you will perform; or as if you are being put through an assault course with a reward at the end if you get over all the obstacles without grumbling. I can think of no answer in the world to give to that mother or to her son. I would like to believe that, in the greater context of what we may know and experience after death, all this suffering will seem less important, less total; and in a strange way, the beauty of their love and courage makes me think I see something like light breaking through – but no pat answers, no book of rules. They confront together all the pressures of the absurd, as mankind has always had to confront them. Nothing anyone can say can make them less real.

   In the conflict of meaning against meaninglessness, the scales are fairly evenly balanced. The only answer isn't really an answer at all: you have to tot up your own equation and work out which, in the end, seems most real to you. For the Christian, the figure at the centre of that equation is a crucified man, the very source of all Being suffering with and for mankind; plus that strange, worrying promise that life is to be trusted, that if we wrestle through the night, in the end the stranger will bless us. At the heart of the tension is stillness and mystery; in the middle of the battle, a silence. The Christian should be centred in that stillness, that mystery, that silence; poised there, he senses, though he cannot yet see, the answer.

8 The truth will set you free

The Christian poised in the middle of contradiction and paradox. Dante's *Divine Comedy* begins with the words, 'In the middle of the road of life, I found myself in a dark wood, where the straight road was lost.' It is not an idea that appeals to us; we are all very civilised nowadays, and the thought of getting lost in the woods is frightening – we like to know exactly where we are. But earlier on we said that you have to lose yourself in order to be able to find yourself – meaning, perhaps, that all the confusion, paradox, ambiguity, questioning, doubting, worrying, searching, which we find so distasteful and long to be rescued from, may be in themselves the very treasure we are seeking. Even where I've tried to find answers in this book, I'm not really satisfied with them. I stick by what I said at the beginning, that I don't want to be a comforting old nanny (even if it would multiply sales), but I want to suggest that we should all have the courage to seek our own solutions – actually to dare to let go in trust, and to let ourselves be lost in the dark wood.

And there is healing there as well as confusion. I resort to Shakespeare here, because I want to talk of intimate and precious truths that are best conveyed in poetry and story. A theme that runs through many of Shakespeare's plays is of people being lost in a strange place, and after confusion, contradiction and error, finding their real selves. It is on the storm-racked heath in *King Lear* that Nature reverses hierarchies and that every character capable of rebirth seizes the chance; the blinded Gloucester can 'see feelingly', his disowned son proves himself a prince, the uncrowned Lear finds true majesty for the first time. Lear begins the play in power and state, but it is only when all his trappings and dignity have been taken from him, when he has been through madness and the storm-blasted heath, that he finds

169

any sort of answer to his first haunting question, 'Who is it that can tell me who I am?', can see people as they really are, and can find the real meaning of love.

The same question brings the characters of *As You Like It* to the forest of Arden in a sort of pilgrimage. They lose themselves there amidst a complex of emotions of bewilderment, ambiguity (a man is in love with a boy, who's really a girl, who's really a boy; a girl is in love with a boy who's really a girl, who's really a boy) joy, mirth, atonement, guilt, remorse, exquisite pleasure, love, all blended together and producing a magical harmony at the end as people realise who they really are, and who the others really are.

> Then there is mirth in Heaven
> When earthly things made even
> Atone together.

The forest becomes like a church, where people find atonement and love.

At the end of *A Midsummer Night's Dream* Theseus dismisses all the strange stories of what happened to the lovers in the wood:

> . . .I never may believe
> These antique fables, nor these fairy toys.

His wife is not so sure – maybe there's more to it all than overwrought imaginations:

> But all the story of the night told over,
> And all their minds transfigur'd so together,
> More witnesseth than fancy's images,
> And grows to something of great constancy,
> But, howsoever, strange and admirable.

At the end all the characters are brought together, but with none of the questions resolved. Out of the darkness step the 'airy nothings' who compounded all the mischief in the first place; but they are here to bless the house and the sleeping lovers. Finally all depart except Puck, who tells us that perhaps the whole play has been a dream:

> If we shadows have offended

Think but this – and all is mended.
That you have but slumber'd here
While these visions did appear.
And this weak and idle theme,
No more yielding but a dream . . .

In the dark places of the wood we lose our way, lose all the external trappings of our identity, lose ourselves, until all that is left is the quest. And in the end maybe it was all a dream, maybe we imagined half the things we thought were real and important, or maybe there was something more there than we realised or could understand. In Shakespeare's terms, those who are prepared to lose themselves in the wood, find themselves – but they must be there, without a backward look, experiencing everything up to the hilt.

Montaigne said, 'The greatest thing in the world is to know how to belong to ourselves', and Karl Jaspers said that philosophy is the responsibility of man as man – that its task is to remind every individual that he *can* be *himself*, and that he ceases to be a man if he relinquishes that privilege. Perhaps that is the basic question this book has been trying to explore. We have looked at some of the many ways in which we try not to belong to ourselves – all the different flights from the consequences of our own being. The truly religious quest plunges headlong into the dark wood in search of God, Being, meaning; in search of oneself – is there any difference? But all our training, all our culture, warns us to hold back. Is it surprising that most popular films and TV serials deal with any time or place rather than the one we live in? Nostalgia for the Thirties, science fiction, tycoons in America, passionate comings and goings in a motel near Birmingham . . . We protect ourselves and get on with life, putting up all the defensive barriers at our disposal, hoping to find happiness but more probably doomed, as Schopenhauer said, to 'vacillate eternally between the two extremes of distress and boredom'. And our answer to everything is so often, 'Why bother' or 'So what?' or 'Why should I?' or 'What's in it for me?'

Let those be the last questions I try to answer, starting

with, 'What's in it for me?' Answer – zilch, zero, a big fat nothing. Actually that's a lie, because there *is* something, and Albert Schweitzer put his finger on it: 'The only ones among you who will be really happy are those who sought and found how to serve.' The point is that if you start the quest in order to get something out of it for yourself, you are going to go terribly wrong. It is only as by-products of self-transcendence that happiness and self-actualisation can result. If you are dedicated to the cause, the quest, or involved in the work of love, your very reaching beyond yourself frees you to experience happiness, to grow, and to live.

Perhaps I can best try to explain this or remove it from the level of generalisation by talking about sex and sex therapy. I know a Christian book isn't the usual place for this, since we are so neurotically obsessed with everything below the belt that we go pale at the very mention of the word sex unless it is hedged in by at least four hundred moral codes and we promise not to enjoy it too much, and only to do it to make babies, but man's approach to sex is a helpful mirror of his approach to God and to life.

To start with, sex is something we have in common with the animal world. As with 'being', so sex can be more or less human, more or less animal. Our first experience of sex is at the level of reducing tension when we masturbate; all that matters is that the tension should be relieved, ideally in the most pleasant way possible. Our approach to life can be very similar; we relieve our anxiety at the challenge of existence by diverting our energies into the group, our career, possessions, drink, drugs, sex or whatever. And religion can become a means of reducing tension – it has no real outward goal but is directed towards the relief of one's own feelings. If you blunder into some church where 'the Spirit' has taken them over and they are all swaying around, arms raised, with beatific smiles on their faces, the similarity to auto-eroticism is unmistakeable. They are getting off on God.

The next stage is when we relate our sexual needs to another person, but here again there are problems if we only see the person as a means to an end or as an object, not an individual in his or her own right. And this is where all the troubles start concerning impotence, frigidity, premature ejaculation and so on. We feel the need to perform, to prove ourselves, to be a fantastic lay. But we don't really know or care who the other person is as long as we can get something out of him or her, and we feel we have to live up to our/his/her/society's expectations. Our very desire and anxiety for pleasure can lead to the pressure and fear that make sex impossible or disappointing. It's the same in our approach to life: we want something out of it and we want something from other people, so we never really see life or people in their own right. They are always part of our devouring needs, be it for support, love, success, sex or whatever. And it's the same with God. We want everything from him – eternal life, forgiveness, love, acceptance, strength, a better job . . . and maybe we work hard at the bargain, being terribly *good* and spending hours in prayer and good works, but as with uninvolved sex, so with life and so with God – it's really just another form of masturbation. We do it for what we get out of it, yet in the end it's all self–defeating because we have surrounded ourselves with objects from which to get pleasure, including a dead God, but nothing that can rescue us from the tyranny of our desires.

The last stage of sex is when it is in the service of something more than itself, when it is the vehicle or expression of a relationship and/or love. No longer is the partner a means to an end – he or she is the end in him- or herself. And there is a commitment that makes us vulnerable – we allow ourselves to be lost with another, in trust. That lostness, that letting go in trust, that commitment to the mutual quest, can bring intense pain, but also intense joy. Sex is no longer masturbating or performing on another body, but an encounter with another person in his or her own right, a celebration of his or her uniqueness, a special language. A mature approach to life and to other people should move along the same lines, in terms of commitment and dedication, of opening and giving oneself rather than demanding and using, of not being afraid simply to be oneself and to appreciate each individual in his or her own right. And it's the same with God. We give up using him for

nice feelings or for what we can get out of him, including
hope of eternal life. Instead, God is an experience that we
encounter in its own right. whose mystery we explore as it
calls us to explore our own.

One of the most moving events I have ever witnessed was
at a sex-therapy session where the counsellors were trying to
help couples in which the husband had become impotent or
the wife frigid. Part of the therapy was for each couple, very
slowly and quietly, to wash each other's feet. Slowly you
could see the fear and tension easing as they recognised that
the body which had failed to pleasure them or with which
they had failed to perform, was actually just the outer casing
of the human individual that they loved. Sex wasn't a hoop
to be jumped through or a performance to be achieved with
maximum bravado, but an expression of a relationship that
didn't even need to be genital. It's when you can accept
yourself, life and God (Being) on that level of openness and
with that absence of demand that life itself opens up in all its
abundance. If I now draw up a list of the ideal qualities for
such a life, it's with the proviso that none of us can ever
reach such a level – but nonetheless the ideal is there, calling
us on.

It starts, as we have already said so many times, with
acceptance of oneself, despite all one's shortcomings and
deviations from the ideal. Just as a child looks at the world
with wide, uncritical eyes, simply noting and observing, so
we look at ourselves and others. We don't complain about
trees because they are green, or water because it is wet, and
it is in the same unquestioning way that we should accept
and love human nature in ourselves and others. 'Homo sum:
humani nil a me alienum puto', wrote Terence: 'I am a man,
so I consider nothing human as alien to me.' Because you
have compassion for yourself, you can have compassion for
your fellow man. Indeed, because you actually feel good
about yourself, you can afford to let people get close to you
and to have deep human relationships (although probably
only with a limited number of people because deep involvement takes time and commitment). Again, because you're
not fooling yourself about yourself, you don't have to filter
reality through a mask, or shelter behind fantasies or

fanaticism. You can accept reality in all its ambiguity and diversity, because you accept yourself in your ambiguity and diversity.

And just being alive is good! Sometimes it's like being a child again, just to stop and look with awe and wonder and joy at a sunset, a flower, a baby. This continued freshness of appreciation means that each moment of life is a gift – not an ordeal. Because life is good, and because we feel good about ourselves, we end up trusting ourselves and becoming self-determining, so that rather than relating everything to what our culture or group demands we get on with the business of living our own lives, relying on our own standards of behaviour and values. But although we feel ourselves to be autonomous, we appreciate the rights of others, we are willing to listen and learn from them, and we respect their uniqueness and difference. We have already called it humility – an awareness of one's own worth without the need to maintain outward 'dignity', status or prestige of age, class, or rank; and a willingness to serve others without concealed demands for love or approbation.

Does all this sound too good to be true? But why should it be? The vital question is to *care*, to take one's life seriously. Leonardo da Vinci said that 'movement is the cause of all life'; if you don't move, you're dead. If you move, perplexing and bewildering though it may be to stumble through the dark wood, you may live, grow and become real. And what calls us into the wood? Sartre spoke about man creating or sculpting himself, but that's too like the Indian rope trick or trying to pull yourself up by your own shoe-strings. Where does the initial call or impetus come from – what is the questioning that goads us into action? Is it the voice of God? And if someone has started on the journey, then who gives a toss whether he knows that it is Being that is calling him, so long as he remains faithful to the call? To ignore the search for meaning in one's life is to ignore the fundamental quality that distinguishes man from the animals. The agonised search for meaning in life isn't a human flaw, but an achievement. And we are free agents, as any existentialist would agree, but we are also responsible – we are committed to something more than ourselves – because we are called by something transcendent that sounds through us. There is that unique 'ought to be' for each individual, that can't be explained by moral laws or super-egos or social conscience: it is the call of being from Being itself.

And how does the Church fit into all this? Well, as we have said, it could actively encourage people to face and accept their real selves, and so to grow. Most of us live in large centres of population that are completely impersonal. We are surrounded by people we don't know and in front of whom we feel we have to play a part. 'Hello, how are you?' Smile, look pleasant. 'I'm fine, thanks. How are you?' 'Oh, fine thanks.' Smiles repeated. The transaction completed, we go our separate ways, untouched by genuine emotion. We live in relative comfort, follow familiar routines, but we seem to have lost touch with all that really matters about our humanity, and have become frightened to experience or express basic human feelings.

The Church that is *not* going to help us in such a situation is the one that deflects all our energies from actually daring to be human, and converts them into good works and pious aspirations for some never-never land in the future. Nor will the Church help that keeps emphasising the wonderfulness of God and the awfulness of man – we feel awful enough already, without having our faces ground in the mud.

No, the Church we need must be modelled more on the client-therapist relationship of total acceptance. You may have wondered how on earth one could ever become the ideal figure I have described on page 174 and elsewhere – this loving, autonomous, creative, unblinkered, generous individual – and the easiest explanation is that people who have a positive attitude to themselves and to the world are the way they are because they were brought up in an atmosphere of basic trust. As children, they knew that they were accepted and loved, liked, wanted and able: the sort of acceptance that was described in a previous chapter as ideal maternal love.

If you haven't experienced that kind of acceptance, your vision of God and the Church that will best match your inner feelings of being unacceptable or having to win acceptance, may be the God-out-there sort, big on sin and good works, or perhaps just full of people and clergy who are terrified to be themselves and terrified of the real world. But there is another way. Even if we haven't been brought up in basic trust, it is never too late to learn new ways forward. That's how the client-therapist relationship works: for possibly the first time in the client's life, he is able to dare to be himself. It is an extremely intimate relationship, person to person, where the client gradually realises, as trust builds between them, that he or she is of unconditional worth, of value no matter what his or her condition, behaviour or feelings. Because the client is accepted unconditionally, he or she is able to explore strange, uncharted and previously dangerous feelings in him- or herself, and is able to live through aspects of past experience that were blocked from consciousness because they were unacceptable, threatening or damaging. Gradually the client comes to realise, as he lives through many widely varying feelings in all their degrees of intensity, that he *is* all these feelings. His behaviour becomes more constructive as he realises that he no longer needs to fear what experience may hold, but can welcome it as a part of his changing and developing self.

I have made much of the client-therapist relationship of total, unconditional acceptance and the healing effect it can have, because for me it is like a microcosm of what the whole Christian journey is about. Even if we haven't been brought up in trust of ourselves and the world, and even if our initial religious experiences are anti-life (I speak as one who was so racked by guilt as a teenager that I became a religious maniac – anything to appease God or thank him for being so totally wonderful as to forgive me for something I couldn't help anyway – viz. puberty, then later on trying terribly hard to be good in order to keep my soul nicely polished for heaven), I think/hope/pray that we can reach a level of self-acceptance and harmony that mirrors our place in creation. There *is* no Father to placate or win approval from, no deadly game of heaven and hell; there is life to be lived, light to be kept burning against the darkness, and trust to be learned. Our deepest relationship to Being is like that of a baby to its mother; underlying everything there is a

sense of acceptance, nurturing, feeding, calling to growth.
Something in life – loss, another person, suffering, restlessness, joy – makes us stand still; and there in the stillness is
the call.

That, for me, is the start of the journey. Einstein once said
that to be religious is to have found an answer to the
question, What is the meaning of life? If you accept that,
then faith and belief are, at base, a simple trust in the
ultimate meaning of existence.

And that's what the Church should reflect. What would it
be like if people could actually come to a place where,
perhaps for the first time, they didn't have to win love or
approval, or do anything useful, or say they believed in
anything, or jump through any of the 1001 hoops the Church
usually sets up – but could just stop and simply *be* and know
that that was enough, that they were loved and accepted
regardless of who or what they were, and forgiven if they felt
the need for forgiveness? Is this wildly unrealistic? I hope
not, because it's what the cross says to me, and I can't
understand the nature of God in any other way. Without
that as its starting-point, the religious life seems not just
pointless, but dangerous.

St Irenaeus said, 'The glory of God is a living man, and
the life of man is the vision of God.' In other words, forget
the glory, heaven, angels, harps, and God sitting on a golden
throne – or if you want to put it more firmly, quote my friend
in the prologue, because that's the sort of God and set-up
she was telling to get lost – and concentrate on the reality of
the glory of God here and now, in every living, breathing
human individual, and the vision offered us by a man who
surrendered everything in the cause of love. That's where
the glory is – in those grotty old late-night supermarkets;
where the meat looks tired and the people even tireder in
Wormwood Scrubs where we sat round a table with a 'lifer'
talking about how he could spend the next twenty years; in
the dirty, back-street church in Fulham where I celebrated
the Eucharist for six or seven elderly, decrepit people and
the church almost trembled with the presence of mystery.

'The glory of God is a living man': it has also been
translated as 'a man fully alive', and obviously we're not

talking about heartbeats and respiratory functioning; as
we've already noted, you can die as a unique personality at
thirty, yet carry on going through the motions of being
human until your physical death. But the glory of God is in
the person who is fully alive, open to Being, taking risks,
growing into all that is in him to be. And this is where the
Church really needs to take stock of itself, because at
present it shows no evidence of being in a position of basic
trust with God from which growth can start. We're still at
the level of contracts and bargaining – of wanting something
from God, rather than accepting him quite simply as he is –
and of keeping him at a safe distance by showing in our
behaviour and rituals that we are not acceptable. In other
words, it's as if we're still at the second stage of sexual
development – we have to play a part because we want
something from the other person, and we don't trust or
know him or her well enough simply to be ourselves. This
comes across in so many different ways: in the great
emphasis on sin and the fallen nature of man, in the
emphasis on sacraments, ritual and priestcraft (ways of
channelling God and/or protecting ourselves from the full
impact), and in the emphasis on *niceness* in the Church. We
all feel that we have to keep those great big Christian smiles
plastered on our faces until the cheek muscles ache with the
effort, but what has this teeth-baring rictus got to do with
real loving, real caring?

The third stage is to stop pretending and bargaining. It's
no longer a question of 'If I'm good will you promise to
forgive/save me?' or 'Life is terrible; get me out of here'; it is
to do with exploring the mystery of another's being, as
he/she explores yours. In a relationship of total acceptance
with another human being, we dare to confront our reality.
It's the same with God. I know it's a highly personal image –
that I'm using word pictures again – but somehow personal
images seem to fit best when describing our relationship to
Being; as if relationship, like suffering, can be the channel of
all that is best and most real in us. Small wonder that the
great spiritual writers talk of the deepest mysteries in terms
of God as mother, father, lover, husband, pursuer, pursued.
We are naked before him, but instead of trying to hide our

stretch-marks, spindly legs, acne, birthmarks or beer guts,
we slowly come to realise that we are beautiful and loved.
And oh the freedom of not having to pretend or buy love
any more. But oh the risk of daring to let ourselves be
naked, when we would like to cover our shame, our lack of
self-worth, with good deeds, ritual, priestly hierarchies, and
smiles. But naked we must be, and that includes the painful
stripping away of our demands for certainty, knowledge,
reward. How can we really love someone if we start by
telling them what we want them to be, what we want them to
do?

No one can deny that the stripping-away process is
painful. As we have seen, one of the strong pulls of
Christianity is that one expects to find there certainty and a
safe anchorage. I vividly remember my feelings of despair,
rejection and anger when I arrived at Oxford as a Christian
with a 'simple' faith, to be confronted with all the weight of
Biblical criticism; one by one the 'certainties' around which I
thought my faith was built were peeled away. I suppose I
went through a number of common reactions, first of all
refusing to accept the findings and searching everywhere for
arguments to combat them – even if they were arguments
that I knew, at base, were flawed. Then I tried shutting my
eyes to it all, perhaps hoping that it might go away if I
ignored it. The last reaction was to become totally nihilistic:
'All right, if it's all uncertain and difficult, throw the lot out
and be cynical about everything.'

But there is another way forward, difficult and painful
though it may be, and that is to learn to accept and live with
the realities of the situation – that life is infinitely complex,
with no easy answers or black and white certainties; life is
ambiguous, and almost all its accepted 'truths' are relative.
You have to find your way with difficulty, and the religious
life is not an arrival at a fixed point, but the starting of and
sticking to a quest. The loss of certainty may be exactly the
place where growth can begin, as we are forced to question
and work out exactly what matters. As to the other questions – 'So what?', 'Why bother?' – I'm not sure we can say
anything helpful: 'Because you risk losing all that is most
precious in our existence as humans'? or 'Because man isn't

a sublimated ape but a repressed angel, and the more you repress the restlessness of your spirit the nearer to being a sublimated ape you will become'? People have to find out for themselves, when their time of questioning comes. Pray God there's someone there then to be with them, who can give them space, silence and acceptance to help them on their way.

Meantime, for us, an absolute commitment is called for: commitment to the journey, to the work of sacrificial love, even though the way is unclear. We must be 'half sure and wholehearted', as someone said, or, as T.S. Eliot put it, our route is about 'hints, followed by guesses: and the rest is prayer, observance, discipline, thought and action'. You need discipline to love, and discipline to create. A friend of mine who is a concert pianist once played me the Grieg concerto he'd been performing on a European tour. I was bowled over. 'Oh you're so lucky to be able to play the piano like that,' I stupidly gushed, to be met with a blank stare and the acid remark that if I thought practising six hours a day for fifteen years could be called luck, then he supposed he was lucky. Hints and guesses, prayer and observance; not to be 'good' to satisfy some heavenly examiner, but because mystery and silence and the desert and the reviving grass-lands of prayer are our matrix, the crucible in which we are refined to our essentials; and discipline, thought and action, because that wholehearted commitment to something less devouring than our own ego is the road to the creation of the true self. The uncertainty, the anxiety, are the very things that can save us from the great *I am* – using religion for our own ends – and help us on the way to serving God for nothing.

I've thought so much about my widowed friend – in a sense, she's been one of my companions through this book, and what I feel now is that when she said, 'Fuck God', shocking though it may sound, it was actually a genuine prayer. A real relationship involves anger, hurt and resent-ment, and trusting the other person with your openness and lack of pretence; it's not easy, but 'the truth will set you free'. In her openness and trust of God, in her daring to be

real, lay the seeds of a relationship that would surely lead to
life; and I know that her daring to be free set something free
in me, began the slow toppling of that idol, uninvolved and
watching, needing to be appeased and bargained with. I
don't think that I loved God simply for himself, nor that I
felt he loved me simply for myself – we were caught in a
contract of 'you scratch my back and I'll scratch yours'
fuelled by my needs, my lack of trust in him or myself, my
refusal to wait and simply let him be, and simply let myself
be. The woman I went to 'help' ended up helping me; she
was the priest, and I the one she ministered to.

'To venture causes anxiety, but not to venture is to lose
oneself.' We have looked at some of the methods we use to
escape from the anxiety of existence, including religion. But
true religion is about learning to be human, to be free, not to
have to be driven by our compulsions, society or God, but to
be responsible for our own existence, choosing where to
make our stand in the cause of meaning versus meaninglessness, living life to the full rather than running away into the
group, the fantasy, the Church, the obsession, the off-
licence, to the pill bottle. Schiller said, 'Spricht die Seele, so
spricht, ach, schon die Seele nicht mehr' – 'when the soul
tries to speak it is soon the soul which is no longer talking.'
The poor clergy feel themselves obliged to act out in public
in a symbolic way the love that is most private and central to
their being. If only the Christian world could learn to speak
through silence, through the quality of its mystery and
being. The louder we talk, the less we believe, the less real
our journey becomes.

Have there been any answers? Once again, and as Jung
suggested, the meaning and purpose of a problem doesn't lie
in its answer, but in our beavering away at it. The meaning
and purpose of our lives come not from the goal, but in the
striving towards that goal, and when the guiding principles
of our lives are directed towards an objective reality beyond
ourselves, then we move from being ego-centred to ego-
transcending – 'unselfed', as Iris Murdoch calls it, and yet
most truly ourselves.

Just as Christ met people where they actually were –
leprous, blind, desperate, failed, alone, dead to the world –

and called them into newness of being, so we are met by the call of Being. And either we follow the long winding road from birth to grave in a stupor – stumbling along full of dreams and longing but never really knowing who we are – or we stop and dare to listen to the question and promise of God, dare to wrestle with the stranger until he blesses us. I have no answers for anyone, but the answer is there for each of us if once we let reality hit us: this is *me*, this is where I am, this is what I am called to be. Going on our journey, living it, experiencing it, *being* it to the full; struggle, suffering, sorrow, joy, laughter, mistakes, failure, new beginnings, hope, peace – trust. The meaning is there, if we dare to face the questions.

Ask me why I am a Christian and I say, 'I don't know.' What called me into the cloud of unknowing, into the dark wood? Because I want to find out who I am? Because I want to know how to love? All I know is that the quest is risky and painful and often feels as if it means wearing a crown of thorns, and yet there is something there . . . light at the end of the wood, I think, I trust. There's a Japanese poem that reads:

> The world of dew is
> A world of dew, yet even
> So, yet even so . . .

It's that maddening, intangible 'yet even so . . . ' that draws one on; and there is more here than can be comprehended by all those alien philosophies – communism, materialism, nihilism, narcissism – that seem to dominate our lives. Those who set off in search of the 'yet even so . . . ' are called by Being, even if they don't know it. To those whose search does not include the symbol of God, the Christian owes respect, silence and support. Anyone searching for the ultimate meaning of life deserves respect and acceptance, even if he does not want to hazard that unseen, further step up the mountain; isn't it enough for us to love him instead of making demands on him?

Knowing that we are loved without question, what greater

joy or pain or privilege than to love the world without question, all that it is, all that it might be? Isn't that what the Church, the body of Christ, is good for? And loving God for nothing, loving the mystery of Being, finding ourselves as we search for him; what other real meaning is there to this short span of life we are given than to seek the answer to the questions of man and Being, of man and God? The question that the cross asks us, and whose answer we will never find until we have shouldered it all the way we are asked to go.

Epilogue

There is a monastery in the mountains of Spain that is a place of pilgrimage for many people. There you will find a beautiful church, and souvenir shops and cafés. Near the church is a steep hill which the monks long ago made a Calvary. At the summit of the hill you can make out a large cross. If you leave the crowded centre and set off up the hill, you find a winding upward path with, at intervals, carved representations of Christ's last journey through Jerusalem, carrying his cross to the place of execution.

Sometimes the path is boring and gloomy, sometimes it's a hard slog straight up-hill, slippery underfoot and easy to stumble; at times you wonder if it's worth the effort, and whether to turn back and rejoin the people below; at other times it's hard to tell if you're going in the right direction, and the path gets overgrown, shrouded by dark trees. Sometimes the going is light and easy, and you come upon beautiful vistas through the trees, down over the hills and valleys around you. Occasionally you come upon other people finding their way up the hill, who give you a hand or a smile, or may be able to tell you what's around the next corner. At other times you meet people who have turned round and are trying to find their way back down again. But you keep on, determined to find out what lies at the top, getting your bearings where you can from the cross at the top of the hill, which sometimes seems to emerge through the trees like a beacon. You're not quite sure why you started the climb or whether it's worth it, and sometimes the solitude is lonely and sometimes it is reviving. But you keep on, because something in you wants to know what's there.

Eventually you reach the top, and there in front of you is a huge figure of Christ on the cross, with Mary and John at his feet. You wait in front of it, tired by the climb, awed by the silence and the suffering. Then it is time to leave, but the path leads on beyond the cross, and there for the first time the whole heart-stopping vista of the hills and mountains and valleys opens out before you. The path takes you gently downhill, back to the people where you started, but their raucous voices, their holiday mood and unconcern, which seemed so jarring before, seem important now – these people *are* the beloved ideas made flesh. The same figure that called you up the Calvary hill is there amongst the people, but perhaps now it's easier to discern his face in theirs, a little easier to understand what this whole heart-breaking, life-giving business is about. His name is Love.